Contents

Introduction

When you hear the term 'heart disease', what do you think? What do you consider to be the biggest threat to your health? Maybe you think that heart disease is not your problem, and you consider that cancer and accidents cause the most deaths. Well, let's look at some facts:

- Heart disease is the number one killer in the United Kingdom.

- Heart disease is responsible for one in four premature (before the age of 75) deaths in men and one in five premature deaths in women in the UK.

- Over 266 million prescriptions are issued for heart disease in England each year.

- 95% of people who die from heart disease have at least one risk factor.

- Many people do not even know they have a heart problem.

These statistics make it very clear, if we have a heart, heart disease is our problem.

Through my family and friends, I have been living with heart disease for nearly three decades. For many years, I have researched, written and taught about the workings of the human body. I became especially interested in heart disease when my father was diagnosed, then my two closest friends, and then my mother-in-law. Over 30 years, I have seen some amazing changes in heart disease management and I have come to understand that everyone has the ability to take some control of their own heart health. I have learned that through nutrition, lifestyle and exercise choices, we can protect the health of our hearts. If we are diagnosed with heart disease, we can work with our health-care providers to minimise the severity of our condition. I have understood how important it is for everyone to take heart disease seriously, and that it is essential for everyone to take action. Using my knowledge, expertise and experiences, I have written this book to inform and empower every person with a heart to take control of their futures.

In this book, I want to teach you about your heart. I wrote this book for everyone. It is a guide for you if you wish to assess your risk for heart disease and minimise it; it provides information and advice for you if you already know you are at risk for heart disease; it is here to help you if you have been diagnosed with heart disease; and it will provide support for your family.

Fortunately, heart disease is a problem that you can deal with. The purpose of this book is to show you how. The first step towards understanding your heart and heart disease is to create a heart profile. Chapter 1 of the book explains how to do this. It explains the structure and functions of your heart. It discusses what can go wrong and encourages you to establish a partnership with your physician to help you set personal goals for your heart. Chapter 2 introduces you to risk factors for heart disease. It includes information that can help you find out your risk for heart disease. For those who develop heart disease, chapter 3 discusses the symptoms and chapter 4 familiarises you with and informs you about the methods of diagnosis. In chapters 5 and 6, the book provides you with the latest medical information about medications and interventions for heart disease. Chapter 7 provides you with vital information on how to cope with a heart attack. Chapter 8 encourages you to take some control of your condition through correct lifestyle choices, and chapter 9 provides advice on how you can live a healthy, happy life with heart disease. Chapter 10 discusses the special needs of women in relation to heart disease. A glossary of terms is included at the back of the book, as well as a list of useful resources.

The book is written in an easy-to-read style and provides you with basic information on each topic. It is filled with checklists and charts to prompt your actions towards ensuring your heart, with or without disease, will remain as healthy as possible in the future.

The book recognises that every person is different. One size does not fit all, especially not for your heart; after all, it is your heart. Everyone has their own set of risk factors, symptoms, or degree of disease severity to address. This book provides you with information to enable you to select the right diet, exercise and treatment plan to suit you. It will inform, encourage, support and empower you if you suffer from heart disease, believe you are at risk, or love someone who is.

A damaged heart can damage your life by interfering with enjoyable activities and even your ability to do simple things, such as taking a walk or climbing steps. But it doesn't have to. I hope this book teaches you about your heart, helps you recognise that heart disease is a real problem, but encourages you to understand that it can be dealt with.

Disclaimer

This book is for general information about heart disease. It is not intended to replace professional medical advice. It can be used alongside medical advice, but anyone with concerns about their risk for heart disease or an existing heart condition is strongly advised to consult their health-care professional.

Whilst every care has been taken to validate the contents of this guide to the time of going to press, the author advises that she does not claim a medical qualification. The reader should seek advice from a qualified medical practitioner before undertaking any particular course of action of treatment.

Chapter One

What is Heart Disease?

You cannot live without your heart. Your heart is a pump and as with all pumps it can become clogged, break down and need repair. When this happens, you have heart disease. To protect your heart, it is critical that you know how your heart works. With a little knowledge about your heart and what is good or bad for it, you can prevent heart disease, or manage it if you have already been diagnosed.

The heart

How your heart works

A normal heart is a strong muscular pump. It weighs between 200 and 425 grams (7 and 15 ounces) and is about the size of your fist. Your heart has four chambers. The upper chambers are called the left and right atria, and the lower ones are the left and right ventricles. A wall of muscle called the septum separates the left and right atria and the left and right ventricles (see the diagram overleaf). Your heart sits between your lungs in the middle of your chest. Your heart is a muscle, and to function your heart needs a continuous supply of oxygen and nutrients, which it gets from the blood that is pumped through the coronary arteries.

'With a little knowledge about your heart and what is good or bad for it, you can prevent heart disease, or manage it if you have already been diagnosed.'

Why is your heart important?

Your heart pumps blood to the organs, tissues and cells of your body, delivering oxygen and nutrients to every cell and removing carbon dioxide and waste products made by those cells. Oxygen-rich blood is carried from your heart to the rest of your body through a complex network of arteries, arterioles and capillaries. Oxygen-poor blood is carried back to your heart through veins.

The left ventricle is the largest and strongest chamber in your heart. It can push blood into your entire body. The right two chambers of your heart (right atrium and right ventricle) pump blood from your heart to your lungs, so blood cells can pick up a fresh load of oxygen in exchange for the waste they've collected during their trip around your body. The oxygen-rich blood returns to the left chambers of your heart (left atrium and left ventricle), which then pump it around the rest of your body.

As blood travels through your heart, it moves through a series of valves. The valves open and close to let blood flow in only one direction.

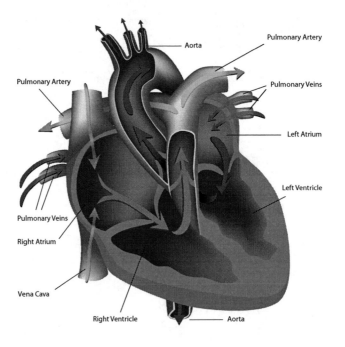

Your heartbeat

A healthy heart makes a lub-dub sound. This sound is your heartbeat, and it is the sound of the valves in your heart closing as your heart pumps your blood. Your heartbeat is controlled by a natural pacemaker called the sinoatrial node (SAN) which is located in the right atrium. This produces electrical impulses which spread over your heart. The SAN normally generates electrical impulses that are carried by special conducting tissue to the atria and ventricles. These electrical impulses cause your heart to pump.

The SAN generates electrical impulses more than once per second to produce a normal heartbeat of 72 beats per minute. The average heart beats about 100,000 times each day and pumps about 7,200 litres (1,900 gallons) of blood.

When something goes wrong

Heart disease includes a number of problems affecting your heart and the blood vessels that bring oxygen and food to your heart. Heart disease is a general term that refers to any disease or condition of your heart, including coronary artery disease, disorders of the heart valves, conduction disorders – heart arrhythmias, cardiomyopathy, heart infections, heart failure – and congenital heart defects.

Coronary artery disease (CAD)

Coronary artery disease (CAD) is the most common type of heart disease and is the leading cause of heart attacks.

When you have CAD, your coronary arteries become hard and narrow as plaque builds up inside them. Plaque is made up of fat, cholesterol, calcium and other substances found in your blood. When plaque builds up in your arteries, the condition is called atherosclerosis. The build-up of plaque occurs over many years.

Over time, plaque hardens and narrows your coronary arteries. This limits the flow of oxygen-rich blood to your heart muscle.

Eventually, an area of plaque can rupture (break open). This causes a blood clot to form on the surface of the plaque. If the clot becomes large enough, it can mostly or completely block blood flow through a coronary artery.

CAD can lead to angina and heart attack.

- Angina is chest pain or discomfort that happens when your heart does not get enough blood. It may feel like a pressing or squeezing pain, often in your chest, but sometimes the pain is in your shoulders, arms, neck, jaw, or back. It can also feel like indigestion (upset stomach). Angina is not a heart attack, but having angina means you are more likely to have a heart attack.

- A heart attack occurs when an artery is severely or completely blocked, and your heart muscle does not get the blood it needs to function for more than 20 minutes.

Heart valve disease

Heart valve disease is a disease in which one or more of your heart valves don't work properly. Birth defects, age-related changes, infections or other conditions can cause one or more of your heart valves to not open fully or to let blood leak back into the heart chambers. This can make your heart work harder and affect its ability to pump blood.

Heart valves can have three basic kinds of problems:

- Regurgitation, or backflow, occurs when a valve doesn't close tightly. Blood leaks back into the chambers rather than flowing forward through your heart or into an artery. Backflow is most often due to prolapse. Prolapse is when the flaps of the valve flop or bulge back into an upper heart chamber during a heartbeat.

- Stenosis occurs when the flaps of a valve thicken, stiffen or fuse together. This prevents the heart valve from fully opening. As a result, not enough blood flows through the valve. Some valves can have both stenosis and backflow problems.

- Atresia occurs when a heart valve lacks an opening for blood to pass through.

You can be born with heart valve disease, or you can acquire it later in life. Heart valve disease that develops before birth is called congenital heart valve disease. Congenital heart valve disease can occur alone or with other congenital heart defects.

Congenital heart valve disease usually involves valves that don't form properly. These valves may not have enough tissue flaps, they may be the wrong size or shape, or they may lack an opening through which blood can flow properly.

Acquired heart valve disease usually involves valves that are normal at first; disease can cause problems to develop over time.

Conduction disorders – heart arrhythmias

Problems with signal conduction, due to disease or abnormalities of the conducting system, can occur anywhere along your heart's conduction pathway. Abnormally conducted signals, resulting in alterations of your heart's normal beating, are called arrhythmias. Heart arrhythmias are changes in the beat of your heart.

An arrhythmia may occur for one of several reasons:

- Instead of beginning in the SAN, the heartbeat begins in another part of your heart.
- The SAN develops an abnormal rate or rhythm.
- The signal bypasses the normal conduction pathway.
- You have a heart block and the flow of the electrical signal within your heart is blocked.

Many arrhythmias occur in people who do not have underlying heart disease. The vast majority of people with arrhythmias have nothing to fear. They do not need extensive exams or special treatments for their condition.

In some people, arrhythmias are associated with heart disease. In these cases, heart disease, not the arrhythmia, poses the greatest risk to the patient.

In a very small number of people with serious symptoms, arrhythmias themselves are dangerous. These arrhythmias require medical treatment to keep the heartbeat regular. For example, a few people have a very slow (bradycardia) or fast (tachycardia) heartbeat. These patients may have symptoms such as chest pain, shortness of breath, lightheadedness or fainting because their heart is not pumping enough blood to the body. If left untreated, their heart may stop beating and these people could die.

Cardiomyopathy

Cardiomyopathy is a disease that changes the structure of the muscle tissue in your heart, or makes it weaker, so it's less able to pump blood efficiently. Angina and arrhythmia are warning signs of cardiomyopathy.

Cardiomyopathy may be either:

- Primary – no specific cause can be identified.
- Secondary – causes can be identified, such as high blood pressure, heart valve disease, artery diseases or congenital heart defects, as well as disease affecting organs other than your heart. Alcohol and drug use (both street drugs and medical drugs) can also cause cardiomyopathies.

Heart infections (endocarditis)

Endocarditis is an infection of the inner lining of your heart chambers and valves. This lining is called the endocardium. Endocarditis starts if your endocardium has been damaged, injured or infected.

There are two kinds of endocarditis:

Infective endocarditis (IE) is caused by bacteria or fungal infections. These cause inflammation and damage your heart cells. The infection reaches your heart through your blood. Once the infectious agent reaches your heart via the blood, it tends to concentrate around the valves. Despite the name, IE isn't contagious. IE can affect people who have normal heart valves but mainly affects people who have:

- Damaged or artificial (manmade) heart valves.
- Congenital heart defects.
- Implanted medical devices in the heart or blood vessels.

Certain factors make it easier for bacteria and fungi to enter your bloodstream. For example, poor dental hygiene and unhealthy teeth and gums increase your risk for infection. Other risk factors include using intravenous (IV) drugs, having a catheter (tube) or another medical device in your body for long periods, and having a history of IE.

In non-infective endocarditis, damage to the endocardium may not be caused by infection. This can happen in conditions such as:

- Congenital heart valve disease.
- Systemic lupus erythematosus (an autoimmune disease).
- Chronic infections like tuberculosis and pneumonia.
- Lung cancer.
- Having had a previous bout of rheumatic fever.

Heart failure

Heart failure occurs when your heart is not able to pump blood through the body as well as it should. This means that other organs, which normally get blood from your heart, do not get enough blood. It does not mean that your heart stops. Signs of heart failure include:

- Shortness of breath (feeling like you can't get enough air).
- Swelling in the feet, ankles and legs.
- Extreme tiredness.

Congenital heart defects

Congenital heart defects are problems with your heart's structure that are present at birth. These defects can involve:

- The interior walls of your heart.
- The valves inside your heart.
- The arteries and veins that carry blood to your heart or out to your body.

Congenital heart defects change the normal flow of blood through your heart. There are many types of congenital heart defects. They range from simple defects with no symptoms to complex defects with severe, life-threatening symptoms.

Congenital heart defects are the most common type of birth defect. They affect 8 of every 1,000 newborns. Many of these defects are simple conditions that are easily fixed or need no treatment. A small number of babies are born with complex congenital heart defects that require special medical care soon after birth.

Over the past few decades, the diagnosis and treatment of complex defects has greatly improved. As a result, almost all children who have complex heart defects survive to adulthood and can live active, productive lives.

Most people who have complex heart defects continue to need special heart care throughout their lives. They may need to pay special attention to how their condition may affect certain issues, such as employment, pregnancy and contraception, and other health issues.

Protecting your heart

To protect your heart from heart disease, or manage your heart disease if you have been diagnosed, you must gather some information and create your personal heart profile. Start by seeing your doctor for a thorough check-up.

- Tell your doctor you want to keep your heart healthy and need help to achieve that goal.
- If you already have heart disease, make sure your treatment plan is appropriate.

'To protect your heart from heart disease, or manage your heart disease if you have been diagnosed, you must gather some information and create your personal heart profile. Start by seeing your doctor for a thorough check-up.'

- If you do not understand something your doctor says, ask for an explanation in simple language. You may want to write down the doctor's instructions.

Questions to ask your doctor

Getting answers to the following questions will give you vital information about your heart. You may want to take this list to your doctor's office:

- What is my risk for heart disease or worsening of my existing heart disease?

- What screening tests for heart disease do I need? How often should I return for check-ups for my heart health?

- What is my blood pressure? What does it mean, and what do I need to do about it?

- What are my cholesterol numbers? (These include total cholesterol, LDL or 'bad' cholesterol, HDL or 'good' cholesterol and triglycerides). What do they mean, and what do I need to do about them?

- What is my body mass index (BMI) and waist measurement? What do they mean? Do they indicate that I need to lose weight for my health?

- What is my blood sugar level? What does it mean?

- What can you do to help me stop smoking?

- How much physical activity do I need?

- What is the best heart-healthy eating plan for me? Should I see a registered dietician or qualified nutritionist to learn more about healthy eating?

- How can I tell if I'm having a heart attack?

Your heart profile

Complete the following table to help create your heart profile. If you *don't know* the answers to some of the questions, ask your doctor for help.

Question	Yes	No	Don't know
Do you smoke?			
Is your blood pressure 140/90 mmHg or higher, or have you been told by your doctor that your blood pressure is too high?			
Has your doctor told you that your LDL (bad) cholesterol is too high, or that your total cholesterol level is 5mmol/l or more, or that your HDL (good) cholesterol is less than 1.2mmol/l?			
Has your father or brother had a heart attack before age 55, or has your mother or sister had one before age 65?			
Do you have diabetes, or do you need medicine to control your blood sugar?			
Are you over 55 years old?			
Do you have a body mass index (BMI) score of 25 or more?			
Do you get less than a total of 30 minutes of moderate-intensity physical activity on most days?			
Has a doctor told you that you have angina, or have you had a heart attack?			

If you answered yes to any of these questions, you should talk to your doctor about the next steps that are appropriate for you.

Summing Up

- Your heart is a pump that pushes blood around your body to supply your cells with food and oxygen and remove their waste.

- Your heart is a muscle that gets energy from blood carrying oxygen and nutrients.

- Having a constant supply of blood keeps your heart working properly.

- Heart disease is a group of conditions affecting the structure and functions of your heart.

- You can protect your heart by keeping a heart profile. This may help you prevent heart disease or make heart disease manageable if you have already been diagnosed.

Chapter Two

Risk Factors for Heart Disease

You can reduce your risk of heart disease by making changes in your lifestyle. Some risk factors are related to others, so making a few changes may help you in many ways. There are no guarantees that a heart-healthy lifestyle will keep heart disease away; however, making these changes is important as they will improve your overall physical and emotional wellbeing.

What are risk factors?

Risk factors are conditions or habits that raise your risk of heart disease. These risk factors also increase the chance that existing heart disease will worsen. There are many known risk factors for heart disease. You can control some risk factors, but not others. The risk factors you can control are called modifiable risk factors because you can modify or change them to protect yourself. The risk factors you cannot control are non-modifiable because you cannot do anything about them.

Modifiable risk factors

High blood pressure

High blood pressure, also known as hypertension, affects 32% of men and 27% of women in the UK. It is a major risk factor for heart disease. High blood pressure is often called a 'silent killer' because you can't see it and you can't feel it; it has no warning signs or symptoms. But you can control it. If you know and control your blood pressure, you can cut your risk of heart attack by up to 25%.

If your blood pressure is too high you may be at risk for heart disease or a heart attack. High blood pressure can damage blood vessel walls and cause scarring. The scarring can promote the build-up of fatty plaque (atherosclerosis) and lead to coronary artery disease. High blood pressure also strains the heart and eventually weakens it. Knowing your blood pressure numbers is important, even when you're feeling fine. If your blood pressure is normal, you can work with your doctor to keep it that way. If your blood pressure is too high, treatment may help prevent damage to your heart.

What is blood pressure?

Blood pressure measures how strongly blood presses against the walls of your large blood vessels (arteries) as it is pumped around your body by your heart. Blood pressure is measured as 'systolic' and 'diastolic' pressures. 'Systolic' refers to blood pressure when your heart beats and pushes blood out. 'Diastolic' refers to blood pressure when your heart is at rest between beats. You can have your blood pressure measured by your GP or at your pharmacy.

'If you know and control your blood pressure, you can cut your risk of heart attack by up to 25%.'

Your blood pressure numbers will be written with the systolic number above or before the diastolic number, such as 120/80 mmHg. The mmHg is millimeters of mercury, these are the units used to measure blood pressure.

What is high blood pressure?

The blood pressure chart from the Blood Pressure Association (www.bpassoc. org.uk) shows ranges of high, low and healthy blood pressure readings. To work out what your blood pressure readings mean, just find your top number (systolic) on the left side of the blood pressure chart and your bottom number (diastolic) on the bottom of the blood pressure chart and read across and up until the two meet. Then refer to the table.

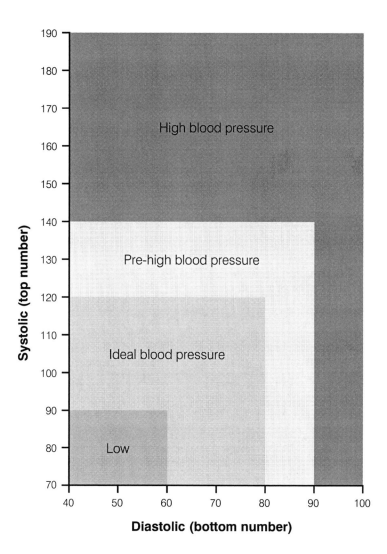

Blood pressure reading	What it means	Action
Ideal blood pressure	Your blood pressure reading is ideal and healthy.	Follow a healthy lifestyle to keep it at this level
Pre-high blood pressure	You have a normal blood pressure reading but it is a little higher than it should be	Make healthy changes to your lifestyle
High blood pressure	You may have high blood pressure (hypertension)	Change your lifestyle and see your doctor

One high reading does not necessarily mean you have high blood pressure. If you have one high reading, you should have your blood pressure measured at least two more times on separate days to check whether it is consistently high. Keep a record of your blood pressure readings.

Cholesterol

Cholesterol is a soft, waxy substance found among the fats in your bloodstream and in all your body's cells. It is important for the healthy functioning of your body. Your body makes cholesterol and you consume it when you eat food from animals like milk and cheese. Your body can also make cholesterol from foods that do not contain cholesterol such as coconut fat, palm oil and trans fats, often used in foods such as crisps, cakes and biscuits.

Cholesterol is carried through your blood by particles called lipoproteins: low-density lipoprotein (LDL) and high-density lipoprotein (HDL). High levels of LDL increase your risk of heart disease and heart attack, as they can increase the build-up of cholesterol in your artery walls causing atherosclerosis. HDL reduces the risk of heart disease, as it carries cholesterol away. Estrogen, a female hormone, raises HDL cholesterol levels, partially explaining the lower risk of heart disease seen in women before menopause.

Triglyceride is the other most common type of fat in the body. Normal triglyceride levels vary by age and sex. But if you have heart disease you are likely to have high levels. High levels of triglyceride combined with high levels of LDL cholesterol speed up atherosclerosis, increasing your risk for heart disease and heart attack.

Your cholesterol levels are dependent on your age, sex and lifestyle choices, and will vary over time. You should get your cholesterol tested every three to five years, more often if you have high cholesterol levels. Refer to the table below which shows the recommended total cholesterol, LDL and HDL levels for healthy adults (www.bbc.co.uk/health/)

Total cholesterol	5.0 mmol/l or less
Low-density lipoprotein (LDL)	3.0 mmol/l or less
High-density lipoprotein (HDL)	1.2 mmol/l or more
Total cholesterol/HDL ratio	4.5 or less

If you have heart disease, or are known to be at risk for heart disease, your total cholesterol should be less than 4.0mmol/l and your LDL cholesterol should be less than 2.0mmol/l

Diabetes

Diabetes is a problem associated with the way our bodies use digested food for energy. Most of the food we eat is broken down into glucose, a form of sugar in the blood. Glucose is the body's main source of fuel. After digestion, glucose enters the blood. Then glucose goes to cells where it is used for energy. However, a hormone called insulin must be present to allow glucose to enter the cells. Diabetes develops when your body does not make enough insulin, or the cells in your muscles, liver and fat do not use insulin properly, or both. As a result, the amount of glucose in your blood increases while your cells are starved of energy. Over time, high blood glucose levels lead to increased deposits of fatty materials on the inside walls of your blood vessels and atherosclerosis. This causes heart disease, which is a leading cause of death among people with diabetes. If you have diabetes, you are twice as likely to have heart disease as someone who does not have diabetes.

While diabetes itself is a risk factor for heart disease, your chances of heart disease are increased further if you are also obese, have abnormal blood cholesterol levels, have high blood pressure and if you smoke.

If you have diabetes you can monitor the effect it is having on your heart by measuring your ABCs.

- A stands for A1C – a test that measures blood glucose control. Your A1C target should be below 7% and your blood glucose targets should be 90-130 mg/dl before meals and less than 180 mg/ml 1 to 2 hours after the start of a meal.

- B is for blood pressure. Your blood pressure target should be less than 130/180 mmHg.

- C is for cholesterol. If you have diabetes your LDL should be less than 2.5 mmol/l.

Overweight and obesity

If you have an obese body, you have too much fat. Too much fat, especially around your waist, can cause high blood pressure, diabetes and heart disease. You may become obese if you eat more calories than you use.

If you are obese, you have more body mass. This increased mass means you have more blood. This extra blood must be pumped around your body. Pumping the extra blood around your body can cause strain on your heart. This strain on your heart is often doubled when you exert yourself and increase your heart rate, as the blood flowing through your heart is too much for it to handle.

If you are obese you may also have high blood pressure, as more body fat means more fatty molecules (such as cholesterol) are in your blood vessels. These fats narrow your blood vessels so your heart has difficulty pushing blood through them. This narrowing worsens the strain on your heart because the heart has to work extra hard to push blood through your narrow blood vessels.

If you are obese you are at risk of heart failure because your heart is overworked. You can experience heart failure through a heart attack as your heart muscle may die as it is not being supplied with oxygen because its blood flow is blocked through a fat-clogged blood vessel. You may also experience heart failure through cardiac arrest, when your heart suddenly stops beating as it has been overworked.

The amount of fat in your body is measured by your body mass index (BMI) which compares your height and your weight. For a quick determination of your BMI (kg/m2), use the following chart (www.bhf.org.uk). Use a straight edge to help locate the point on the chart where height and weight intersect. Read the number in the box at this point. For example, an individual who weighs 68kg and is 1.66m tall has a BMI of 25. (To work this out divide weight in kgs by square of height in metres.) Then, refer to the table overleaf to indentify your risk of heart disease.

BMI Chart

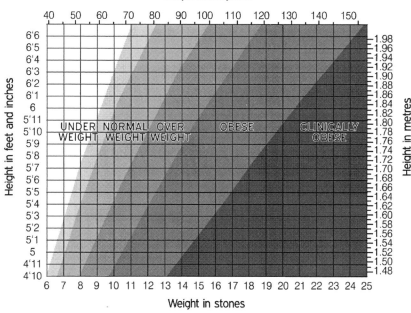

Classification	BMI (kg/m2)	Risk of developing heart problems
Underweight	Less than 18.5	Increased
Normal weight	18.5-24.9	Least
Overweight	25.0-29.9	Increased
Obese Class I	30.0-34.9	High
Obese Class II	35.0-39.9	Very high
Obese Class III	40.0 or more	Extremely high

'Getting regular physical activity may reduce "bad" cholesterol, increase "good" cholesterol and lower high blood pressure.'

For persons 65 years and older the 'normal' range may begin slightly above BMI 18.5 and extend into the 'overweight' range.

Obesity is also measured by the size of your waist. Waistlines in women that are greater than 35 inches are considered high risk for obesity and heart disease. Men should measure 40 inches or less to remain healthy.

Physical inactivity

If you are physically inactive, you are not getting the recommended level of regular exercise. Physical inactivity can double your risk of dying prematurely from heart disease. Getting regular physical activity may reduce 'bad' cholesterol, increase 'good' cholesterol and lower high blood pressure. It can also protect your heart by helping to prevent and control diabetes. Finally, physical activity can help you lose or maintain your desired weight.

Alcohol

You may have heard that drinking alcohol, particularly red wine or beer, is good for your heart. There is some evidence that people who drink moderately have a somewhat lower risk of heart disease than those who do not drink or who drink excessively. Small amounts of alcohol may raise HDL cholesterol, lower blood pressure, stop the formation of blood clots which may prevent heart attacks and prevent artery damage caused by LDL cholesterol. But until we know more about the effects of alcohol consumption, you should not drink alcohol specifically for the health of your heart. In fact, drinking too much of any type of alcohol can increase your blood pressure and contribute to the development of heart disease.

Smoking

You probably know that cigarette and tobacco smoking increases your risk of lung cancer, but it also greatly increases your risk of heart disease.

Research has shown that smoking increases your heart rate, narrows your major arteries and can create irregularities in the timing of your heartbeats, all of which make your heart work harder. Smoking also raises blood pressure. Although nicotine is the main active agent in cigarette smoke, other chemicals and compounds, like tar and carbon monoxide, are also harmful to your heart. These chemicals lead to the build-up of fatty plaque in the arteries, possibly by injuring the vessel walls. And they also affect cholesterol and levels of fibrinogen, which is a blood-clotting material. This increases the risk of a blood clot that can lead to a heart attack.

Cigarette smoking increases your risk of heart disease. When it acts with high blood pressure, high blood cholesterol, physical inactivity, obesity and diabetes, it increases your risk even more.

For help giving up smoking take a look at *Stop Smoking – The Essential Guide* by Simon Daubney, Need2Know 2012.

Stress

Stress is considered a risk factor for heart disease, although the effects of stress on the heart are not completely understood. Living a stressful life can cause you to adopt poor habits like smoking and eating badly, but stress itself can affect your heart in several ways:

- During times of stress, your nervous system releases certain chemicals called hormones (most often adrenaline). These hormones raise your blood pressure and can injure the lining of your arteries. When your arteries heal, the walls may harden or thicken, making it easier for plaque to build up.

- Stress increases the amount of blood clotting factors that circulate in your blood, making it more likely that a clot will form. Clots may then block an artery narrowed by plaque and cause a heart attack.

- Stressful situations raise your heart rate and blood pressure, increasing your heart's need for oxygen. If you already have heart disease, this need for oxygen can bring on angina or chest pain.

Non-modifiable risk factors

Non-modifiable risk factors that contribute to heart disease are risk factors for heart disease that you cannot do anything about. However, you can assess your total heart disease risk by understanding how non-modifiable risk factors for heart disease affect you.

Age

Heart disease is more likely to occur as you get older. About 85% of people who die as a result of heart disease are 65 years of age or older.

Gender

Men have a greater risk for heart disease and get heart disease earlier than women on average. After menopause, a woman's risk for heart disease increases, but does not reach the level of a man's.

Family history

If your parents had heart disease at an early age, you are at increased risk for heart disease. If your father had a heart attack before age 55 or your mother had a heart attack before age 65, your risk for coronary artery disease is increased.

Ethnic background

If your ethnicity is First Nations, African or South Asian background, you have a higher risk for developing heart disease. This increased risk is partly due to higher rates of high blood pressure, obesity and diabetes in these populations.

Summing Up

- You can reduce your risk of heart disease by being aware of your risk factors. Become aware of your personal risk for heart disease.

- A heart health assessment or cardiovascular risk assessment is available to anyone over the age of 40. This is a health check or assessment carried out by your GP or practice nurse to find out your risk of heart disease.

- Once you know your risk, start to follow a healthy lifestyle to prevent or control you risk factors for heart disease. Make the changes gradually, one at a time.

- Making them is very important.

- Take action today to protect your heart.

'You can reduce your risk of heart disease by being aware of your risk factors. Become aware of your personal risk for heart disease.'

Chapter Three

Symptoms of Heart Disease

Each type of heart disease has different symptoms, although many heart problems have similar warning signs. The symptoms you experience depend on the type and severity of your heart condition. You should learn to recognise your symptoms and the situations that cause them. Always call your doctor if you begin to have new symptoms or if existing symptoms become more frequent or severe. Early recognition and treatment of heart disease is vital.

What is a symptom?

A symptom is a problem that you may notice or feel. There are several classic symptoms of heart disease which when recognised can lead to an early and accurate diagnosis. These symptoms include shortness of breath, chest pain, palpitations, dizziness, fainting, fatigue, blue colouration to your skin or oedema. If you have heart disease you may not have all these symptoms and some symptoms that suggest you have heart disease may be due to another cause. However, the presence of any of the symptoms discussed in this chapter should be viewed as a possible early warning to seek advice from your doctor.

Shortness of breath (dyspnea)

Shortness of breath, also termed dyspnea, is the feeling of having difficult or laboured breathing. It is the earliest and most common symptom of heart disease. However, you must remember that we all experience shortness of breath sometimes, so if you are experiencing shortness of breath it is important to decide whether it is related to heart disease or not.

Shortness of breath *not* related to heart disease can result from:

- Lung disease, which narrows or stiffens the airways making it difficult for air to get into and out of the lungs (pulmonary dyspnea).

- Anxiety, which can cause hyperventilation. The most severe example is the shortness of breath you may experience during a panic attack. It may feel difficult to get air in (functional dyspnea).

Shortness of breath may be considered a symptom of heart disease (cardiac dyspnea) if it is inappropriate to the activity you are performing. It is normal to feel short of breath after walking up a flight of stairs or running. It is not normal to feel short of breath after routine walking, walking a few steps or while at rest. Another sign of heart disease is when shortness of breath begins suddenly. The abrupt onset of shortness of breath may be due to heart failure.

Cardiac dyspnea usually occurs when your heart is pumping too little blood. This may happen if:

- The ability of your heart to function as a pump is weakened by coronary artery disease.

- Blood flow through your heart is prevented by damage to a valve between your heart's pumping chambers.

If your heart is pumping too little blood, blood and fluids begin to back up. This backed-up fluid puts pressure on your heart and lungs, and fluid begins to leak from your bloodstream into your lungs, a condition called pulmonary oedema or pulmonary congestion. This will cause you to feel short of breath.

In the early stages of heart disease, cardiac dyspnea may occur only during physical activity. As heart disease worsens, cardiac dyspnea will occur with less and less activity and eventually when you are resting. Cardiac dyspnea at rest occurs mostly when you lie down because fluid seeps throughout your lungs. This symptom often occurs at night and is then called nocturnal dyspnea. If you have nocturnal dyspnea you should sleep propped up by pillows to avoid lying flat as gravity causes fluid to collect at the base of the lungs, reducing your symptoms.

Chest pain

Chest pain is the second most common symptom of heart disease. But not all chest pain is due to heart problems.

Chest pain *not* related to heart disease may be due to:

- A pulled muscle in the wall of your chest.
- Irritated joints.
- Pinched nerves.
- Heartburn caused by reflux of stomach acid.
- Panic attack.
- Pericarditis when the membrane of the heart becomes infected.

Chest pain related to heart disease may be due to:

- Angina, which occurs when your heart muscle does not receive enough oxygen to function properly due to plaque formation in the coronary arteries that supply the heart with blood and oxygen. When your heart's demand for oxygen becomes greater than the supply, pain fibres are stimulated and chest pain occurs. Activities that may increase your heart's need for oxygen include exercise and stress which cause your heart to beat faster, or after a big meal when blood and oxygen are diverted from your heart to your stomach and intestines to digest your food. When your coronary arteries are very narrow, angina may occur at rest or after minimal activity. The pain created during angina is like a pressure in your chest, as if your heart is being squeezed in a vice. It may be confined to the centre of your chest or radiate from the centre of your chest to your shoulders and down your left arm. It may also radiate to your jaw and be confused with a toothache. The pain can last 2-3 minutes but goes away when you are at rest.

- A heart attack which occurs when one of your coronary arteries becomes completely blocked by cholesterol and a clot. The pain of a heart attack is similar to angina but lasts longer and does not go away with rest. The pain may be accompanied by sweating, nausea and a feeling of anxiety or dread. Some heart attacks may be 'silent' in that you cannot feel them, but usually the pain is severe. A heart attack may occur when you are exerting yourself, but they often occur when you are at rest.

- Sometimes a panic attack may seem like a heart attack. But, if you are over 40 and have any symptoms of a heart attack you should see your doctor immediately.

If you experience chest pain you should always see your doctor so he can decide if it is related to heart disease. Any squeezing, steady pain in the centre of the chest that lasts for more than 2 minutes could be a symptom of heart diseases.

Heart palpitations

Ordinarily, you are probably unaware of your heartbeat. However, when you experience palpitations you may become very aware of your heartbeat and you may feel disturbed by this. Palpitations may feel like fluttering, thumping, flip-flopping, a skipped heartbeat or a pounding in your chest or neck.

Forms of palpitations *not* related to heart disease include:

- Palpitations when you are anxious, along with shortness of breath.
- Palpitations brought on by exercise, eating, smoking, drinking alcohol or caffeine or by taking certain prescription drugs.

Arrhythmias are heart palpitations that may occur if you do not have heart disease but are at risk for heart disease. This may be the case if you experience a series of very rapid heartbeats when you have not been active. You may feel well apart from these palpitations and the palpitations may not last long, but you should see your doctor.

Other arrhythmias may occur if you already have a heart condition. These can make you feel weak and short of breath because your heart is pumping a reduced amount of blood.

Lightheadedness or dizziness

Feelings of lightheadedness or dizziness result in an inadequate blood supply to the brain.

Feelings of lightheadedness or dizziness *not* related to heart disease include:

- Aneamia and other blood disorders.
- Dehydration.
- Viral illnesses.
- Diabetes.
- Thyroid, gastrointestinal, liver, kidney and nervous disorders.

Lightheadedness or dizziness can be a sign of heart disease and result from:

- Conduction disturbances which may make your heart beat too quickly (tachycardia) or too slowly (bradycardia), and either of these situations may result in an inadequate blood supply to the brain, causing you to feel to dizzy or lightheaded.
- Cardiomyopathy.
- Vasovagal syncope is a common cause of dizziness and lightheadedness. The vagus nerve is overstimulated and causes your body's blood vessels to dilate and your heart to slow down. This decreases the ability of your heart to pump blood upwards to your brain. Without blood flow, your brain turns off.

Because so many different conditions can produce these symptoms, if you experience episodes of lightheadedness or dizziness you should see your doctor.

Fainting or loss of consciousness

Fainting usually occurs after your brain has been deprived of blood and oxygen for about 10 seconds.

Reasons for fainting *not* related to heart disease include:

- The vasovagal response. Many people faint when they are frightened as the vagus nerve can temporarily slow your heart rate and decrease blood to your brain.

- After standing still for long periods of time such as soldiers standing to attention or singers in a choir. Blood pools into your legs and there is inadequate blood flow to your heart and then your brain. This can be prevented by changing position frequently.

- An abnormal metabolic condition, such as during diabetes when taking too much insulin may cause your blood sugar levels to drop too low. When this happens your blood is not able to carry enough oxygen to your brain.

- Hyperventilation.

- Hysteria.

- Epilepsy.

Heart disease may also cause you to faint, especially if you have:

- Irregular heartbeats or arrhythmia, in particular a type of arrhythmia called heart block. In this case you have a very slow heartbeat resulting in an inadequate blood and oxygen supply reaching your brain.

- Very rapid heartbeats of more than 150 beats per minute. If your heart beats too quickly there is not enough time for it to fill with blood in-between each heartbeat, which results in inadequate blood and oxygen reaching your brain.

- An obstruction or narrowing of the carotid arteries. These are blood vessels in your neck that carry blood and oxygen to your brain.

- A narrowed valve leading out of the heart.

- A heart attack may result in fainting as your heart muscle becomes weak and temporarily stops pumping.

Lethargy, fatigue or daytime sleepiness

Feelings of fatigue occur because your heart muscle is weakened and unable to pump enough blood and oxygen to your body so it can function normally.

Feelings of fatigue *not* related to heart disease include:

- Anaemia.

- Diabetes.

- Lung and thyroid diseases.
- Undiagnosed depression and stress.

Fatigue related to heart disease will only have started recently. You will begin the day with a normal amount of energy but get increasingly more tired throughout the day until you feel exhausted. This is because your heart muscle is weakened and unable to pump enough blood and oxygen around your body.

Fatigue associated with heart disease is often described as having weak or heavy legs and may occur with or without being short of breath.

Oedema

Oedema is swelling or puffiness of your ankles, legs, eyes, chest or belly. The swelling is due to water retention in the cells of your body.

Oedema *not* related to heart disease may occur due to:

- Swelling in the ankles which can occur if you are not active during the day as gravity results in blood being retained in the legs rather than returning to the heart.
- Varicose veins and other abnormalities in the veins which can result in ankle oedema.
- Kidney and liver disease.
- An allergic reaction to some foods.
- Cancer that has spread to the lymphatic system may cause swelling of the arms and legs.

Oedema is a common sign of heart disease. The site of the oedema gives you clues about problems with your heart:

- Oedema in the belly or legs is associated with a weakened muscle on the right side of your heart and poor pumping quality.
- Oedema in the ankles in the evening after standing during the day may indicate you are retaining water and salt and signal right-sided heart failure.

If the left side of the heart is weakened swelling will build up in the lungs and result in shortness of breath not oedema.

Bluish discolouration of the skin (cyanosis)

Cyanosis is the bluish discolouration of the skin and the membranes in your mouth and nose (mucous membranes). It is caused by a lack of oxygen in your blood, and it usually shows mostly in your lips and fingernails.

Cyanosis not related to heart disease is called peripheral cyanosis and can be seen when your body is exposed to cold temperatures, but it also occurs in people with diseased arteries.

Central cyanosis is a sign of congenital heart disease and severe heart disease. It occurs because there is abnormal mixing of venous and arterial blood. Venous blood is usually blue because it carries blood with little oxygen back to the heart. Arterial blood is usually red as it carries blood with oxygen from the heart to the rest of the body. Venous and arterial blood are normally separate. Central cyanosis occurs when venous and arterial blood are mixed together in the heart.

Symptom	Most common cause	What to do
Shortness of breath	Altered heart function	See your doctor
Chest pain	Coronary artery disease	Call your doctor or go to the emergency department
Palpitations	Extra heartbeats	Abstain from coffee and cigarettes and call your doctor
Fainting	Heart rhythm disturbance	See your doctor
Oedema	Heart disease or abnormalities of the veins	See your doctor
Fatigue	Lack of sleep	Get plenty of rest. See your doctor if you have other symptoms
Cyanosis	Altered heart function	See your doctor

(After Professor Lawrence S. Cohen, Yale University)

Summing Up

- Heart disease is manageable when detected early.

- Simple observation can allow you to recognise the classic symptoms of heart disease summarised in the table on page 40.

- Seeking advice from your doctor can lead to an accurate and early diagnosis, allowing early and effective treatment.

Chapter Four

Getting a Diagnosis

What is a diagnosis?

A diagnosis for heart disease is an attempt to identify the cause and type of heart disease. If you suffer from heart disease, your diagnosis will be made by various health-care professionals including your GP and several specialists that you may be referred to. The diagnostic procedure involves questions about medical history, medical tests and the processing of the answers. Your diagnosis allows decisions to be made about your treatment. Some of the tests used to diagnose heart disease are described in this chapter. Always talk to your doctor about any concerns you have about the diagnostic procedure, the need for any tests, how any tests will be done, the risks or what the results will mean. For more information about any of these tests see www.patient.co.uk and www.webmd.boots.com.

Diagnostic tests for heart disease

Electrocardiogram

An electrocardiogram (ECG) is a test that checks for problems with the electrical activity of your heart. An ECG records your heart's electrical activity as a line drawing on paper.

What it shows

An ECG is done to:

- Look at your heart's electrical activity.
- Find the cause of symptoms of heart disease.

- Check your heart if you have risk factors for heart disease including high blood pressure, high cholesterol, cigarette smoking, diabetes or a family history.

- Find out if the walls of your heart are too thick.

- Check how well a medication or a mechanical device (pacemaker) implanted in your heart is working.

The test

- You may be given a gown to wear and a cover to use during the test.

- You will lie on a bed and the areas on your arms, legs and chest where small metal electrodes will be placed are cleaned and shaved. To help conduct the electrical impulses, a special paste or small pads soaked in alcohol may be placed between the electrodes and your skin.

- Electrodes are placed on the skin of your arms, legs and chest. Leads join the electrodes to a machine that takes readings and traces your heart's activity onto a paper.

- You will be asked to lie still and breathe normally during the test.

- The test takes 5 to 10 minutes.

Understanding the results

An ECG records the electrical activity of your heart and turns it into a line drawing of spikes, curves and dips called waves:

- The P wave shows the electrical activity in the upper chambers (atria) of your heart.

- The QRS complex shows the electrical activity of the lower chambers (ventricles) of your heart.

- The ST segment usually appears as a straight, level line between the QRS complex and the T wave and shows your ventricle is contracting but no electricity is flowing through it.

- The T wave shows that your lower heart chambers are resetting and preparing for their next muscle contraction.

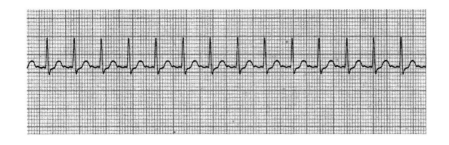

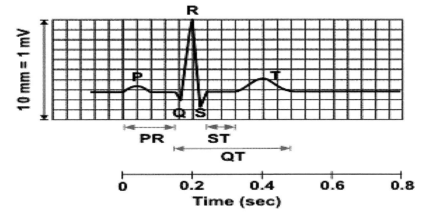

(Reproduced with kind permission, R.E. Klabunde, Cardiovascular Physiology Concepts at www.cvphysiology.com)

ECGs may need to be repeated over several hours or days (serial ECG) to look for changes. In addition to the standard ECG, your doctor may recommend these other specialised ECG tests:

- A holter monitor. This is a portable ECG that monitors the electrical activity of your heart, 24 hours a day for 1-2 days while you go about your normal daily activities. It is most often used when the doctor suspects an abnormal heart rhythm or not enough blood flow to the heart muscle (ischaemia). Electrodes from a monitor are taped to your skin. Once the monitor is in place, you can go home and perform all of your normal activities (except showering or getting it wet). You will be asked to keep a diary of your activities and any symptoms you experience.

An event monitor. This is used if your symptoms are infrequent. This is a device that records and stores a few minutes of your heart's electrical activity when you push a button. Each time you develop symptoms you should push the button on the monitor and try and record your heart's electrical activity. The information is passed to your doctor for interpretation. An event monitor is usually used for one month.

Stress test (or treadmill test or exercise)

Sometimes heart problems can be seen only during exercise or while symptoms are present. An exercise ECG is a test that checks how your heart performs while you exercise on a motor-driven treadmill or pedal a stationary bicycle. This test is sometimes called a 'stress test' or a 'treadmill test'.

A resting ECG is always done before an exercise ECG test, and results of the resting ECG are compared to the results of the exercise ECG.

What it shows

An exercise ECG is done to:

- Help find the cause of unexplained chest pain.

- Help decide on treatment for you if you have angina.

- See how your heart copes during exercise if you have had a heart attack or heart surgery.

- Help find the cause of symptoms that occur when you exercise or are active, such as dizziness, fainting or rapid, irregular heartbeats (palpitations).

- Check for a blockage or narrowing of an artery after heart surgery.

- See how well treatment for chest pain or an irregular heartbeat is working.

- Help you decide how to start an exercise programme if you have been inactive for a number of years and are at risk of heart disease.

The test

- Electrodes are attached to the skin on your arms, legs and chest. These are hooked by leads to a machine that records information and draws your heart activity as lines on paper.

- You will either walk on a treadmill or pedal on a stationary bicycle while being monitored by an ECG machine. The test is usually performed in a series of stages, each lasting 3 minutes. After each 3-minute stage, the resistance or speed of the treadmill or bicycle is increased.

- For the treadmill test, you will walk on a slow-moving, level treadmill. As the test progresses, the speed and steepness of the treadmill will be increased so that you will be walking faster and at a greater incline.

- For the stationary bicycle, you will pedal the bicycle fast enough to maintain a certain speed. The resistance will then be gradually increased, making it harder to pedal.

During the test, your heart rate, ECG and blood pressure will be recorded and you might be asked how hard you feel the exercise is. The test continues until you need to stop, you reach your maximum heart rate, or you begin to show symptoms of stress on your heart and lungs (such as fatigue, extreme shortness of breath or angina) or until the ECG tracing shows decreased blood flow to your heart muscle. The test may also be stopped if you develop serious irregular heartbeats or if your blood pressure drops below your resting level.

When the exercise phase is completed:

- You will be able to sit or lie down and rest.

- Your ECG and blood pressure will be checked for 5 to 10 minutes.

- The entire test usually takes 15 to 30 minutes.

Further tests may be needed to further evaluate an abnormal exercise ECG test result.

Echocardiography

What it shows

Your doctor may perform an echocardiogram, sometimes called an 'echo' to:

* Find out how your heart is functioning.

* Check the ability of your heart chambers to pump blood. Your doctor may calculate the amount of blood pumped out of the left ventricle during each heartbeat (ejection fraction). You might have a low ejection fraction if you have heart failure.

* Determine the presence of many types of heart disease.

* Monitor you if you have heart valve disease.

* Monitor how effective medical or surgical treatments are.

The types of echocardiograms

There are several types of echocardiograms and your doctor will help determine which is best for you.

* Transthoracic echocardiogram: A hand-held transducer is placed on your chest. It transmits high-frequency sound waves (ultrasound) which bounce off your heart structures, producing pictures that can be used by the doctor to detect heart disease.

* Transoesophageal echocardiogram (TEE): A transducer is inserted down your throat into your oesophagus (the swallowing tube that connects the mouth to the stomach) so clear pictures of your heart can be obtained without interference from your lungs and chest.

* Stress echocardiogram: The echocardiogram is performed just before and just after exercise on a treadmill or stationary bicycle. This test can be used to look at the pumping action of your heart when it is stressed.

* Dobutamine stress echocardiogram: This is a form of stress echocardiogram. The stress is produced by giving you a drug that stimulates your heart to make it 'think' it is exercising. It is used to determine

how well your heart performs during activity when you are unable to exercise on a treadmill or stationary bike. It is also used to assess whether you have coronary artery disease.

- Intravascular ultrasound: This is a form of echocardiography performed during cardiac catheterisation (see page 51). During this procedure, the transducer is threaded into your heart blood vessels through a tube (catheter) in your groin.

The test

Transthoracic echocardiogram:

- During the echocardiogram, you will be given a hospital gown to wear. A technician will place three electrodes on your chest. The electrodes are attached to an ECG.

- The sonographer will ask you to lie on your left side on an exam table. He or she will place a sound wave transducer on several areas of your chest. The wand will have a small amount of gel on the end which will help produce clear pictures.

- You may be asked to change positions during the exam in order for the sonographer to take pictures of different areas of your heart. At times, you may be asked to hold your breath.

- The test will take about 40 minutes.

Transoesophageal echocardiogram:

- An IV will be inserted into a vein in your arm or hand so that medications can be given.

- A technician will place electrodes attached to an ECG machine on your chest.

- A dental suction tip will be placed into your mouth to remove any saliva. A thin viewing instrument (endoscope) will be inserted into your mouth, down your throat, and into your oesophagus. You may be asked to swallow to help pass the endoscope. Once the endoscope is positioned, pictures of the heart are obtained.

- When completed, the tube is withdrawn

- The test takes about 10 to 30 minutes and you will be monitored for about 20 to 30 minutes after the test. You should not eat or drink until the anaesthetic spray wears off or until the numbness in your throat is gone (about an hour).

- Arrange for someone to take you home, as you should not drive until the day after the test due to the sedative you will be given.

Dobutamine-induced stress test:

- A technician will place electrodes attached to an ECG machine on your chest.

- An intravenous line (IV) will be inserted into a vein in your arm so you can be given the dobutamine medication.

- The technician will perform an echocardiogram and measure your heart rate and blood pressure while you are at rest. You will be given dobutamine through the IV while the technician takes pictures. The medication will cause your heart to react as if you were exercising: your heart will beat faster and more strongly. You may feel warm and flushed with a mild headache.

- The test will take about 60 minutes. You will not be able to leave until all the symptoms you have experienced during the test have gone.

Nuclear scan

A nuclear heart scan produces pictures of your heart created from the energy released when a safe, radioactive substance called a tracer is injected into your bloodstream and travels to your heart.

There are two main types of nuclear heart scan:

- Single-photon emission computed tomography (SPECT).

- Positron emission tomography (PET). PET can provide more detailed pictures of the heart. However, PET is newer and is less available than SPECT.

What it shows

A nuclear scan is done to:

- Check for coronary heart disease.

- Look for damage to your heart muscle caused by a heart attack, injury, infection or medicine. This is called myocardial viability testing.

- See how well your heart pumps blood to your body. This is called ventricular function scanning.

Two sets of pictures are taken. The first set is taken right after a stress test, while your heart is beating fast. The second set is taken while your heart is at rest.

The test

- You will be given a gown to wear.

- An IV line will be inserted into a vein in your arm so the radioactive tracer can be placed into your bloodstream at the right time.

- Electrodes attached to an ECG machine will be placed on your body to check your heart rate during the test.

- You will perform an exercise or dobutamine-induced stress test as detailed above. Before the stress test stops, the tracer is injected through the IV line.

- The nuclear heart scan will start immediately after the stress test.

- You will lie on a table next to a nuclear heart scan camera or on a table that goes slowly through the hole of a doughnut-shaped camera.

- Two sets of pictures are taken. One will be taken right after the stress test and the other will be taken after a period of rest. It takes about 15 to 30 minutes to take each set of pictures.

- You may be asked to return on a second day for more pictures.

- After the test you can return to your normal activities.

Cardiac catheterisation

Cardiac catheterisation, also called coronary angiogram, is a test to find out if you have atherosclerosis. If you have atherosclerosis, this test can pinpoint the size and location of the plaque that is narrowing your coronary arteries. Results from cardiac catheterisation help determine which treatments may be effective.

What it shows

Cardiac catheterisation checks:

- Blood flow in your coronary arteries.

- Blood flow and blood pressure in the chambers of your heart.

- The pumping action of the heart including how well your heart valves work and if there are defects in the way the wall of your heart moves.

- If a congenital heart defect is present and how severe it is. Cardiac catheterisation can sometimes also be used to help correct the defect.

- Blood flow through the heart after surgery.

Cardiac catheterisation can be used to perform operations such as:

- Coronary angioplasty, whereby a tiny balloon at the catheter tip is inflated to widen narrowed arteries or heart valves.

- Electrophysiological studies and catheter ablation (destruction), whereby a device at the catheter tip is used stimulate your heart and record electrical activity and to destroy heart tissue that may be causing arrhythmias. This is only available in some hospitals.

The test

Before the test you must:

- Arrange for someone to take you home after the test. You may not have to stay in the hospital overnight.

This test is performed by a cardiologist.

- You will be asked to lie on a flat table under a large X-ray machine. Several small metal electrodes connected to an ECG machine will be placed on your legs, arms and chest.

- An IV needle will be inserted into a vein in one of your arms to give you fluids or medicine during the procedure. You will receive a sedative which will make you sleepy.

- A thin, flexible cardiac catheter is usually inserted into an artery in your groin, elbow or wrist. The catheter insertion area will be shaved and cleaned with antiseptic.

- A local anaesthetic will be injected into the skin at the insertion site. The blood vessel at the insertion site is punctured by a special needle so the catheter can be passed in. The catheter is slowly advanced through the blood vessel until the catheter tip can be used to visualise your heart's vessels and chambers. The pictures will be seen on a television or computer screen. Blood and heart tissue samples may also be removed through the catheter.

- A small amount of contrast material will be injected through the catheter into your heart chambers or your coronary arteries. The dye can be seen as it moves through the arteries.

- You may be asked to hold your breath or move your head slightly to provide a good view of the heart and its blood vessels. You may be asked to cough or breathe deeply.

- You may be given medication to help open up or narrow your coronary arteries. You may be asked to breathe into a special mouthpiece to help measure the flow of oxygen in your circulating blood.

- The entire procedure usually takes about one hour.

- After the test, the catheter will be removed from the insertion site and the site may be closed using stitches or a special seal.

- After the test, you will be monitored and sent home either after a short observation period (6 hours) or the next day. Any stitches may be removed within 5 to 7 days.

Computed tomography

What it shows:

Computed tomography (CT scan) combines many X-ray images with the aid of a computer to produce cross-sectional views of your body. Cardiac CT is a heart imaging test used to visualise your heart and blood vessels with or without IV contrast dye. There are several types of CT scans used in the diagnosis of heart disease:

- Coronary CT angiography (CTA): This is a heart imaging test that takes high-resolution, three-dimensional pictures of the moving heart and vessels to determine if plaque has built up in the coronary arteries. An iodine-containing contrast dye is injected into an IV in your arm to improve the quality of the images. A medication that slows or stabilises your heart rate may also be given through the IV to improve the imaging results. The test usually takes about 10 minutes.

- Calcium score screening heart scan: This is a CT scan that is used to detect calcium deposits found in atherosclerotic plaques in your coronary arteries and evaluate your risk for future coronary artery disease. The computer will create a calcium 'score' that estimates the extent of coronary artery disease based on the number and size of calcified coronary plaques in the coronary arteries. The calcium score screening heart scan takes only a few minutes to perform and does not require injection of intravenous iodine contrast.

The test:

- Your doctor will tell you how to prepare for the test, depending on the type of test that is ordered. You may need an IV, blood work or other lab tests.

- You may be required to have nothing to eat and only drink clear liquids after midnight the night before the test. Clear liquids include clear broth, plain gelatin and ginger ale.

- You will change into a hospital gown and lie on a special scanning table.

- An IV may be inserted into a vein in your arm.

- During the scan, you will feel the table move inside a doughnut-shaped scanner. The high-speed CT scan captures multiple images.

- After the scan you may continue all normal activities and eat as usual.

Your results will be examined to determine your risk for future coronary artery disease.

Magnetic resonance imaging

Magnetic resonance imaging (MRI) uses large magnets and radio frequency waves to produce pictures of the inside of your body; you will not be exposed to X-rays. An MRI gives information about your heart as it is beating and creates images of the heart throughout its pumping cycle.

What it shows:

MRI is used to:

- Look at the structure and function of your chest, including your heart, lungs, major vessels and the outside lining of your heart (the pericardium).

- Determine the presence of coronary artery disease, pericardial disease, cardiac tumours, heart valve disease, cardiomyopathy and congenital heart disease.

The test

- If you are afraid of closed spaces (claustrophobic), you may be given medication to help you relax (sedative).

- Remove any metallic or magnetic items (belt buckles, zips, watches, wallets with bank or credit cards that use magnetic strips) as the MRI uses powerful magnets to create its images. Inform the MRI staff if you have any metallic implants or any metal under your skin.

- A gown will be provided.

- A technician will place electrodes attached to an ECG machine on your chest and back.

- An IV line will be inserted into a vein in your arm in order to inject contrast material to make your organs more visible in the pictures.

- The MRI scanner is a long tube that scans your body as you lie on a bed.

- You will lie on your back on the scanner bed. During the exam, you will be asked to lie as still as possible. The technician will ask you to hold your breath for short periods so your breathing movements do not blur the images.

- You will wear headphones or earplugs to muffle the loud banging noises made by the machine.

- The MRI scan takes about 30 to 75 minutes.

- After the test, if you were sedated, your doctor will give you instructions on when you can eat, drink and return to normal activities, and you should be driven home by a companion. If you did not receive sedation, you may resume your usual activities and normal diet immediately.

Summing Up

There are many diagnostic tests that help doctors tell if you have heart disease. Your doctors will recommend which tests are right for you. Make sure you:

- Follow all instructions when preparing for, during and after your tests.

- Tell your doctor or the technician about any symptoms you may be feeling during and after your test.

- Ask your doctor to carefully explain the results of your tests so you understand what they mean for you.

- Follow all treatment your doctor recommends based on the results of your tests.

Chapter Five

Medications

Medications may be needed to help control your risk of heart disease or an existing condition. If you need medication, always take your medication according to your doctor's instructions. Never stop your medication without telling your doctor and always inform them of any changes in your symptoms, any new symptoms and any side effects of the drugs that you may be experiencing. For more information about any of these drugs see www.webmd.boots.com.

Cholesterol-lowering medication

If you have high cholesterol, you are at risk of heart disease. Medication to lower cholesterol may reduce this risk.

Cholesterol-lowering drugs include:

- Statins, which block the production of cholesterol in the liver. They lower 'bad' cholesterol (LDL) and may raise 'good' cholesterol (HDL). Statins have been shown to reduce the risk of heart attacks and death from heart disease.

- Nicotinic acid, which is a B-complex vitamin. Nicotinic acid is found in food, but is also available at high doses by prescription. It lowers LDL cholesterol and raises HDL cholesterol.

- Bile acid resins which bind to bile. Bile is a substance produced by your liver and made largely from cholesterol. Bile acid resins prevent bile from being reabsorbed into your body, so these drugs work by decreasing your body's supply of cholesterol.

- Fibric acid derivatives which reduce the production of triglycerides and can increase HDL cholesterol.

- Cholesterol absorption inhibitors.

'If you need medication, always take your medication according to your doctor's instructions. Never stop your medication without telling your doctor and always inform them of any side effects.'

The side effects of cholesterol-lowering drugs can include:

- Muscle aches.
- Abnormal liver function.
- Allergic reaction (skin rashes).
- Heartburn.
- Dizziness.
- Abdominal pain.
- Constipation.
- Decreased sexual desire.
- Flushing with nicotinic acid.

If you experience any side effects from cholesterol-lowering drugs, tell your doctor immediately.

Diuretics

Diuretics cause your kidneys to get rid of unneeded water and salt which decreases blood volume and makes it easier for your heart to pump.

You may be given diuretics if you:

- Have high blood pressure.
- Swelling and water build-up caused by heart failure.
- Difficulty breathing due to heart disease.

When you take diuretics:

- If you are taking a single dose a day, take it in the morning with your breakfast or right afterwards.
- If you are taking more than one dose a day, take the last dose no later than 4pm.

Follow your doctor's dietary advice which may include:

- Following a low salt diet.

- Including high potassium foods (such as bananas and orange juice) in your diet or avoiding potassium-rich foods, salt substitutes and other dietary sources of potassium, depending on the type of diuretic you are taking.

- Avoiding alcohol and sleep aids.

Side effects of diuretics can include:

- Frequent urination for up to six hours after a dose.

- Extreme tiredness or weakness. This will decrease as your body adjusts to the medication.

- Muscle cramps and thirst.

- Dizziness, lightheadedness when getting up from a lying or sitting position.

- Blurred vision.

- Confusion.

- Headache.

- Sweating.

- Restlessness.

- Dehydration. You can tell if you are dehydrated as you may have dizziness, extreme thirst, an excessive dryness of the mouth, decreased urine output, dark-coloured urine or constipation.

- Fever.

- Sore throat and/or a cough.

- Ringing in the ears.

- Unusual bleeding or bruising.

- Rapid and excessive weight loss.

- Skin rash.

- Loss of appetite, nausea and vomiting.

If you experience any side effects from diuretics, tell your doctor immediately.

Angiotensin-converting enzyme (ACE) inhibitors

ACE inhibitors block the activity of an enzyme called angiotensin-converting enzyme. This blocks the effects of a substance called angiotensin that causes your blood vessels to become narrow. Therefore, ACE inhibitors cause your blood vessels to relax and widen (dilate). This makes it easier for blood to flow through the vessels. There is less back up of blood in your heart and lungs and decreased pressure for your heart's left ventricle to pump against. ACE inhibitors also increase the amount of water and salt (sodium) in your urine.

ACE inhibitors may:

- Relieve your symptoms of heart disease.

- Lower your risk of being hospitalised for heart failure.

- Lower your risk of death if you have a weakened left ventricle and have recently had a heart attack.

ACE inhibitors are one of the first choices in drugs for treating heart failure. You may be given ACE inhibitors if you:

- Are at risk of heart failure.

- Have symptoms of heart failure.

- Have heart failure caused by problems with your left ventricle.

Side effects of ACE inhibitors can include:

- A dry cough (common).

- A rash or itching.

- Allergic symptoms.

- Excess potassium in the body.

- Low blood pressure.

- Kidney problems

- Interactions with other medications.

If you experience any side effects from ACE inhibitors, tell your doctor immediately.

Beta blockers

Beta blockers block the electrical nerve impulses that stimulate your heart. This decreases the activity of your heart and causes your heart to beat with less force.

Beta blockers are often prescribed if you have:

* Heart failure.

* High blood pressure.

* Angina.

* Abnormal heart rhythms.

* Heart attack.

You should:

* Take beta blockers with meals, at bedtime or in the morning. Food delays how beta blockers are absorbed and may reduce side effects.

* Follow your doctor's instructions about how often to take this drug.

Side effects of beta blockers can include:

* Dizziness or lightheadedness, especially when you get out of bed or rise from a chair. Get up more slowly.

* Tiredness.

* Cold hands and feet.

* Headaches.

* Nightmares and difficulty sleeping.

* Heartburn, diarrhoea or constipation and gas.

* Sudden weight gain.

* Increased shortness of breath, wheezing, difficulty breathing.

* Skin rash.

* Slow, fast or irregular heartbeat.

* Swelling of feet and lower legs.

- Chest pain.

If you experience any side effects from beta blockers, tell your doctor immediately. Long-term use of beta blockers can help manage your risks for heart disease or your condition. When you start taking beta blockers your symptoms may become worse while you adjust to the medication. This is a normal effect; once your heart adjusts you will feel better.

Calcium channel blockers

Calcium channel blockers affect the movement of calcium in the cells of your heart and blood vessels. As a result, calcium channel blockers relax blood vessels and increase the supply of blood and oxygen to your heart while decreasing its workload.

Calcium channel blockers are prescribed to treat:

- Angina.

- High blood pressure.

- Heart failure caused by high blood pressure when other medications to lower blood pressure do not work.

You should:

- Take calcium channel blockers with food or milk.

- Avoid alcohol, it may interfere with the effects of calcium channel blockers and increase the side effects.

Side effects of calcium channel blockers can include:

- Drowsiness.

- Increased appetite.

- Weight gain.

- Breathing difficulty, coughing or wheezing.

- Irregular or slow heartbeat.

- Skin rash.

If you experience any side effects from calcium channel blockers, tell your doctor immediately.

Aspirin

Aspirin has been used to prevent and manage heart disease since 1970. Aspirin can:

- Decrease pain and inflammation associated with heart disease. Aspirin blocks the action of an enzyme called cyclooxygenase. When this enzyme is blocked, your body produces less of a substance called prostaglandin. Prostaglandin is is a chemical that signals injury and pain.

- Inhibit blood clots. Some prostaglandins in your blood cause your blood platelets to clump together and form blood clots. When aspirin inhibits prostaglandins, it inhibits the formation of blood clots. Blood clots are harmful because they can clog the coronary arteries leading to your heart and increase the risk of heart attack. Aspirin can reduce your risk of heart attack.

- Reduce heart damage during a heart attack and can prevent the occurrence of future heart problems.

- Reduce your risk of death. Regular aspirin use can reduce death among the elderly, people with heart disease and people who are physically unfit.

You will benefit from aspirin therapy if you:

- Have coronary artery disease or atherosclerosis.

- Have had a heart attack.

- Are experiencing symptoms of a heart attack and do not have a history of aspirin allergy and are advised by emergency personnel to chew one aspirin slowly. Aspirin is especially effective if taken within 30 minutes of the onset of symptoms.

- Have undergone bypass surgery to treat heart disease.

- Have angina.

- Have a risk factor for heart disease or a heart attack.

- Are a man over the age of 50

You should:

- Always speak to your doctor before you begin taking aspirin regularly. An appropriate dose of aspirin is half of the standard 325 milligram aspirin (between 80 and 160 milligrams per day). A baby aspirin containing 81 milligrams or low dose adult aspirin varieties may be right for you.

- Not take aspirin on an empty stomach. Take aspirin with a full glass of water with meals or after meals to prevent stomach upset.

- Not break, crush or chew extended-release tablets or capsules; swallow them whole. Chewable aspirin tablets may be chewed, crushed or dissolved in a liquid.

- Not drink alcoholic beverages while taking this medication. Taking aspirin with alcohol increases the chance of stomach bleeding.

- Not take aspirin in place of other medications or treatments recommended by your doctor

Some common side effects of aspirin include:

- Upset stomach and nausea.

- Nervousness and trouble sleeping.

- Severe stomach pain and heartburn.

- Severe nausea or vomiting.

- Unusual bleeding, such as blood in the urine or stools, nosebleeds, any unusual bruising, heavy bleeding from cuts, black stools, coughing up of blood, unusually heavy menstrual bleeding or unexpected vaginal bleeding, vomit that looks like coffee grounds.

- Facial swelling or asthma which may indicate an allergy.

- Ringing in your ears.

- Severe headache.

- Confusion.

If you experience any side effects from aspirin, tell your doctor immediately.

Nitrates

Nitrates improve the blood flow to your heart. Nitrates can:

- Relieve angina.

- Prevent angina when used before energetic activities that can cause angina (such as sexual intercourse or walking up stairs or a hill).

- Prevent angina that occurs during daily activities (long-term use).

Nitrates come in different forms including pills, sprays, skin patches and skin pastes. Pills and spray forms of quick-acting nitroglycerin help relieve sudden angina. Longer acting pills or skin patches may be used for long-term prevention of chest pain during daily activities.

Side effects of nitrates may include:

- Headache or pulsating in your head.

- Decrease in blood pressure which may make you feel dizzy.

If you experience any side effects from nitrates, tell your doctor immediately.

Digitalis

Digitalis drugs work by making your heartbeat stronger and can help slow down heart rate. They help an injured or weakened heart. Digitalis drugs strengthen the force of your heart muscle's contractions, help restore a normal, steady heart rhythm and improve blood circulation.

Digitalis drugs can be helpful:

- If you have heart failure.

- If you have an irregular heartbeat.

You should:

- Try to take the digitalis drug at the same time every day.

- Follow the label directions on how often to take it. The time allowed between doses and how long you need to take it will depend on your condition. You may have to take the drug for a long time, possibly for the rest of your life.

- Follow your doctor's advice about your diet. He may recommend you follow a low sodium-high potassium diet.

Side effects of digitalis drugs include:

- Loss of appetite, nausea and vomiting.

- Changes in vision, such as flashes or flickering of light, sensitivity to light, seeing things larger or smaller than they are, blurring, colour changes (yellow or green) and seeing halos or borders on objects.

- Drowsiness and fatigue; do not drive a car or operate heavy machinery.

- Headache.

- Confusion.

- Depression.

- Muscle weakness.

- Irregular heartbeat or slow heart rate.

If you experience any side effects from digitalis drugs, tell your doctor immediately.

Summing Up

▓ Some heart medications help prevent heart disease and some treat heart disease.

▓ Always talk to your doctor to find out exactly how and when to take your medication.

▓ Always take your medication as prescribed, never stop taking your medication or change it suddenly.

▓ Stick to a routine, use a pill box marked with the days of the week to help you.

▓ If you are taking medication, check with your doctor before taking over-the-counter medication or natural remedies.

▓ Report any side effects of medications to your doctor.

Chapter Six

Heart Surgery

What is heart surgery?

Heart surgery is surgery on your heart and/or blood vessels. Heart surgery treats complications of heart disease using coronary angioplasty, coronary artery bypass grafting, atherectomy, heart valve replacement and cardiac pacemakers. It also includes heart transplantation. More than 30,000 people have heart surgery in the UK each year. For more information about any of these surgeries see www.patient.co.uk.

Common types of heart surgery

Coronary angioplasty

Coronary angioplasty improves flow of blood to your heart through coronary arteries that have become narrowed. Narrowed or blocked arteries are widened by a balloon and a stent attached to a catheter. A catheter is a thin, flexible tube which is inserted into a coronary artery. A balloon at the tip of the catheter is blown up at the narrowed section of the artery to force it wider. A stent (a small mesh tube) is left in place to keep the artery widened. This procedure allows enough blood to get to your heart to deliver the oxygen it needs to function properly.

Coronary angioplasty may be recommended if you have angina or have had a heart attack. If you have angina, coronary angioplasty can:

- Relieve your angina pain.
- Reduce your need for angina medication.

- Ease symptoms such as breathlessness.

- Enable you to be more active.

- Improve your ability to do everyday activities, such as climbing stairs and walking any distance.

- Reduce your risk of having a heart attack.

- Make you feel generally better so you are more able to do the things you want to do, such as going to work and enjoying a social life.

If you've had a heart attack, coronary angioplasty can:

- Increase your chances of surviving.

- Reduce your chances of having another heart attack.

What to expect

- You lie on a couch in a catheterisation room. An X-ray machine is mounted above the couch. You are given a local anaesthetic. A 'guide' catheter is inserted through a wide needle or small cut in your skin into a blood vessel. The doctor pushes the catheter up your blood vessel towards your heart. Low-dose X-rays are used to monitor the progress of the catheter tip which is manipulated into the correct position.

- The tip of the catheter is pushed inside your coronary artery down to the narrowed section. A second 'balloon catheter', which has a balloon surrounded by a wire mesh stent at the tip, is passed down the guide catheter. The balloon is inflated for 30-60 seconds to open the stent, which pushes against the artery walls. The balloon is then let down and the stent is left to support the artery and keep it open. Blood then flows through your artery more freely.

- During the procedure your heartbeat is monitored by electrodes placed on your chest which provide a tracing on an ECG machine.

- The procedure usually takes around 30 minutes. You will normally be able to go home the day after having a coronary angioplasty. You should avoid any heavy activities such as lifting until the small wound where the catheter was inserted has healed. You should not drive a car for a week after having an angioplasty.

How safe is a coronary angioplasty?

Coronary angioplasties are one of the most common types of heart surgery. Over 61,000 procedures are performed in England each year. Coronary angioplasties are most commonly performed in people who are 65 years of age or older as they are more likely to have angina.

Coronary bypass surgery

Heart bypass surgery can be used to treat heart disease when your coronary arteries are blocked. The blood is given a new pathway to your heart as a blood vessel is removed from one area of your body and placed around the area or areas of narrowing to 'bypass' the blockages and restore blood flow to your heart muscle. The vessel that redirects the blood flow is called a graft.

These substitute blood vessels can come from your chest, legs or arms. They're safe to use because there are other pathways that take blood to and from those tissues. The surgeon will decide which graft(s) to use depending on the location of your blockage, the amount of blockage and the size of your coronary arteries. It is common for three or four coronary arteries to be bypassed during surgery.

What to expect

- Your surgeon will prepare the graft by removing a blood vessel from your leg or lower arm.

- The surgeon will make an incision (about 6 to 8 inches) down the centre of your breastbone to get direct access to your heart. You will be connected to a heart-lung bypass machine, which allows for circulation of blood throughout your body during surgery. Your heart is stopped and the surgeon then performs the bypass procedure. Your heart may be stopped for about 30-90 minutes of the 4-5 hour surgery.

- In some cases, the surgeon may perform surgery while your heart is still beating. The heart-lung machine is not used.

- After surgery, the surgeon closes your breastbone with special wires and your chest with special internal or traditional external stitches.

'Coronary angioplasties are one of the most common types of heart surgery. Over 61,000 procedures are performed in England each year.'

- When you wake up, you will be in the recovery room or an intensive care unit (ICU).

- After 24 hours you will be moved to a ward. You will be encouraged to get out of bed and move around because this helps prevent chest infections and blood clots in your legs. A physiotherapist will visit you regularly to help you do exercises to aid your recovery.

- You can expect to stay in the hospital for about a week.

Minimally invasive heart bypass surgery: keyhole surgery

During minimally invasive bypass surgery, the surgeon performs the surgery through small cuts near your knee to obtain the graft and small cuts in your chest to perform the operation. Your surgeon will advise you if keyhole surgery is appropriate for you.

Atherectomy

An atherectomy is a procedure used to help remove plaque from blood vessels other than coronary arteries. If such vessels become blocked with plaque, blood flow is prevented and death can occur to tissues that have been left with no blood supply.

This procedure can be performed through a surgical operation or with the aid of catheters and lasers

- A surgeon may open your vessels and directly remove the plaque.

- If lasers and catheters are used, a small incision is made in your arm or groin, allowing access to your vessels. Following administration of local anaesthetic and usually some sedation, a small guide wire followed by the catheter, and often laser tip, is passed along your vessel until it reaches the site of the plaque. The plaque can be either cut out or removed using laser technology.

Heart valve replacement

Heart valve surgery is performed to repair or replace a valve in your heart that is leaking or narrowed and not working properly.

There are a number of procedures for repairing or replacing valves. Surgery is commonly required, although there are some newer, non-surgical procedures. Surgical procedures include:

- A commissurotomy to open up valves that have thickened and are perhaps stuck together.

- Annuloplasty to repair a ring of fibrous tissue at the base of your heart valve (annulus).

- A surgeon may reshape a valve by cutting out a section or sections of your valve.

- Decalcification to remove calcium build-up from your valves.

- Replacing or shortening the cords and muscles that support your valves so your valve will be strengthened and able to close properly.

- Repairing holes or tears in your valves with a patch.

- Replacing valves with durable manmade materials, animal tissues or human tissues.

What to expect

- Your heart will be stopped so the surgeons can work on your valve or valves. To ensure your body continues to receive a flow of oxygen-rich blood, you will be hooked up to a heart-lung machine which takes over the pumping action of your heart.

- The surgery can take anywhere from 2 to 4 hours, depending upon the number of valves that need to be repaired or replaced. When you wake up, you will be in the recovery room or an ICU.

- After 24 hours you will be moved to a ward. You will be encouraged to get out of bed and move around. A physiotherapist will visit you regularly to help you do exercises to aid your recovery.

- You can expect to stay in the hospital for about a week.

Alternatives to surgical valve repair: keyhole surgery

- Minimally invasive valve replacement surgery is a procedure where long-handled tools are inserted into your chest through four or more small cuts. While watching a video monitor, the surgeon guides the tools and conducts the surgery.

- Percutaneous valve replacement is a non-surgical approach to valve replacement, that uses long, flexible catheters inserted into an artery (usually in the groin or arm) and threaded through the blood vessels into the heart. Percutaneous valve replacement does not require stopping your heart or the use of a heart-lung machine.

- Your surgeon will advise you if keyhole surgery is appropriate for you.

Cardiac pacemakers

Your heartbeat is controlled by a natural pacemaker through an electrical impulse. You may need to have an artificial cardiac pacemaker if:

- You have a heart block that delays electrical conduction through your heart causing your heart to beat too slowly.

- Your heartbeats are too fast and cannot be controlled by medication.

- You have heart failure which may cause your heart to pump irregularly.

Artificial cardiac pacemakers are reliable and comfortable. They are about the size of a matchbox and weigh about 20 to 50 grams. The artificial cardiac pacemaker is positioned just under your collarbone under the skin and will have one or more leads which are placed into your heart through a vein.

The artificial cardiac pacemaker takes over the role of your heart's natural pacemaker. An artificial cardiac pacemaker has a pulse generator which sends electrical impulses to stimulate your heart to contract and produce a heartbeat. Most artificial cardiac pacemakers work only on demand when they are needed. Others send out impulses all of the time.

What to expect

▓ Artificial cardiac pacemakers are fitted under a local anaesthetic with sedation. After the pacemaker is fitted, you'll usually stay overnight in hospital and your artificial cardiac pacemaker will be checked thoroughly before you leave. Serious complications from artificial cardiac pacemakers are very unusual.

▓ You should be able to get back to your normal lifestyle fairly quickly.

Heart transplant

If you need a heart transplant, it is probably because you have end-stage heart failure. This means your heart is damaged or weakened and can't pump enough blood to meet your body's needs. 'End-stage' means your condition has become so severe that all treatments, other than heart transplant, have failed.

A heart transplant is surgery to remove your diseased heart and replace it with a healthy heart from a deceased donor.

Overview

Heart transplants are a life-saving measure for end-stage heart failure when medical treatment and other surgery have failed. Because donor hearts are in short supply, if you need a heart transplant you must go through a careful selection process. You must be ill enough to need a new heart, yet healthy enough to receive it.

After a heart transplant, you will be put on a lifelong health-care plan. Your lifelong health-care plan will include taking multiple medicines on a strict schedule, watching for signs and symptoms of complications, keeping all medical appointments and stopping unhealthy behaviours (such as smoking). If you carefully follow your doctor's instructions you will probably be able to resume your normal lifestyle; you may even be able to return to work.

Heart transplantation is carried out on a number of sites around the UK:

▓ Papworth Hospital, Cambridge.

▓ Harefield Hospital, London.

'Heart transplants are a life-saving measure for end-stage heart failure when medical treatment and other surgery have failed.'

- Freeman Hospital, Newcastle Upon Tyne.

- Wythenshawe Hospital, Manchester.

- Queen Elizabeth Hospital, Birmingham.

- Golden Jubilee Hospital, Glasgow.

If you have heart failure you will be looked after by cardiologists and specialised heart failure nurses at hospitals around the UK. Many of these will have a link with the nearest heart transplant centre. If the cardiologist feels that you are a candidate for a heart transplant you will be referred for assessment. The decision about whether a heart transplant is right for you will be taken by a team of health-care professionals.

You may not be a suitable candidate for heart transplant surgery if you:

- Are over 70 years old.

- Have poor blood circulation throughout your body.

- Have kidney, lung or liver diseases that can't be reversed.

- Have a history of cancer.

- Are unable or unwilling to follow a lifelong health-care plan after a transplant.

- Have high blood pressure in your lungs that can't be reversed.

- Have an active infection.

If you are eligible for a heart transplant you will be placed on a waiting list for a donor heart.

The heart transplant process

Heart transplant surgery is done in a hospital when a suitable donor heart is found. When a suitable heart from an organ donor becomes available it is allocated to you if you are an appropriate recipient. This depends on the size and blood group of the donor heart. This allocation is organised by NHS Blood and Transplant (www.nhsbt.nhs.uk).

The donor heart

Guidelines on how a donor heart is selected require that the donor meet the legal requirement for brain death and that the appropriate consent forms are signed. A series of precise measurements are made on the function of the donor's heart. If it is suitable it will be removed and stored on ice and transported rapidly to the transplant centre.

In the meantime, as the recipient, you will be anaesthetised and your chest will be opened. A bypass machine will be hooked up to the arteries and veins of your heart. The machine pumps blood through your lungs and body while your diseased heart is removed and the donor heart is sewn into place. There can be no more than 4 hours between the time the heart is removed from the donor and the time it receives your blood supply. With its new blood supply your donated heart restarts and takes over your circulation. At the end of the operation, you will be transferred to the ICU and will stay there for several days before moving on to one of the surgical wards.

After your transplant

You will spend 1 to 2 weeks in the hospital and have 3 months of monitoring by the transplant team at the heart transplant centre. Monitoring may include frequent blood tests, lung function tests, ECGs, echocardiograms and biopsies of the heart tissue. A heart biopsy is a standard test used to see whether your body is rejecting the new heart.

While in the hospital, you may start a cardiac rehabilitation (rehab) program. Cardiac rehab is a medically supervised programme that includes counselling, education and exercise training to help you recover. Rehab may start with a member of the rehab team helping you to sit up in a chair or take a few steps. Over time, you'll increase your activity level.

Although heart transplant surgery is a life-saving measure, it has many risks. Careful monitoring, treatment and regular medical care can help manage some of these risks. The risks include:

- Primary graft dysfunction: This occurs if the new donor heart fails and isn't able to function. Factors such as shock or trauma to the donor heart or narrowed blood vessels in your lungs can cause primary graft dysfunction. Medicines may be used to treat this condition.

- Rejection of the donor heart: Rejection occurs when your immune system sees the new heart as a 'foreign body' and attacks it. Half of all possible rejections happen in the first 6 weeks after surgery, and most happen within 6 months of surgery.

- Cardiac allograft vasculopathy (CAV). CAV is an ongoing disease in which the walls of the coronary arteries in your new heart become thick, hard and lose their elasticity. To detect CAV, your doctor may recommend an annual coronary angiography and stress echocardiography.

Emotional issues and support

Having a heart transplant may cause fear, anxiety and stress. While you're waiting for a heart transplant, you may worry that you won't live long enough to get a new heart. After surgery, you may feel overwhelmed, depressed or worried about complications. All of these feelings are normal. It's important to talk about how you feel with your health-care team, a professional counsellor and family and friends.

Summing Up

▨ Heart surgery is done to correct problems with the heart.

▨ Results of heart surgery are usually excellent.

▨ After heart surgery you will require ongoing care and should take steps to make long-term changes to your lifestyle.

▨ Heart surgery and your lifelong health-care plan can reduce your symptoms, improve your quality of life and increase your lifespan.

Chapter Seven

Getting Help for a Heart Attack

What is a heart attack?

A heart attack is a serious medical emergency in which the supply of blood to your heart is suddenly blocked, usually by a blood clot. The lack of blood to your heart can seriously damage your heart muscle. If blood flow is not restored within 20 to 40 minutes, death of your heart muscle will begin. The medical term for a heart attack is myocardial infarction.

A heart attack is different from cardiac arrest. A cardiac arrest happens when your heart stops pumping blood around your body. One of the causes of cardiac arrest is a heart attack.

Signs of a heart attack

Most heart attacks occur in people with coronary heart disease.

Heart attacks are very common and are one of the leading causes of death in England. Each year in England, an estimated 111,000 people have a heart attack. Many heart attacks that lead to death are preventable. This is because most of the risk factors that cause heart attacks are preventable.

'Many heart attacks that lead to death are preventable. This is because most of the risk factors that cause heart attacks are preventable.'

Symptoms of a heart attack include:

Chest discomfort	Most heart attacks involve discomfort in the centre of the chest that lasts for more than a few minutes, or goes away and comes back. The discomfort can feel like uncomfortable pressure, squeezing, fullness or pain.
Other discomfort	Including pain or discomfort in one or both arms, the back, neck, jaw or stomach.
Shortness of breath	Often comes along with chest discomfort. But it also can occur before chest discomfort.
Other symptoms	May include breaking out in a cold sweat, nausea, light-headedness and an overwhelming feeling of anxiety.

'Over the last decade, death rates from heart attacks in England have fallen by around 25%.'

Many heart attacks start slowly, as a mild pain or discomfort. Your symptoms may come and go. If you have had a heart attack, you may not recognise the symptoms of a second one because the next attack can be different.

If you have heart disease, you should learn the signs of a heart attack. If you are not sure you are having a heart attack, you should still contact your doctor.

Most heart attacks occur in people who are over 45 years of age. Men are two to three times more likely to have a heart attack than women.

Over the last decade, death rates from heart attacks in England have fallen by around 25%. This may be related to a decrease in the number of people smoking cigarettes. However, the number of deaths is still higher than in many other western European countries. It is thought that this is because England has higher rates of obesity, diabetes and physical inactivity than in other countries.

Plan ahead

Make a plan now for what you would do if a heart attack should happen. Doing so will save time and could save your life.

- Learn the heart attack warning signs.
- Think through what you would do if you had heart attack symptoms.

- Decide who would care for any dependents in an emergency.

- Talk with your family and friends about the heart attack warning signs and the importance of acting fast by calling 999.

- Talk to your doctor about your heart attack risk and what you can do to reduce it.

- Talk to your doctor about what you should do if you experience any heart attack symptoms.

- Gather important information to take along with you to the hospital. Do this by preparing a heart attack survival plan. Fill in the form below (adapted from Act in Time to Heart Attack Signs www.nhlbi.nih.gov/actintime), print it out, and keep copies in handy places, such as your wallet or purse.

Heart Attack Survival Plan

Information to share with emergency personnel/hospital staff

Medicines you are taking:

Medicines you are allergic to:

If your symptoms stop completely in less than 5 minutes you should still call your doctor.

_____

Doctor's name:

Doctor's office phone number:

_____

Person you would like contacted if you go to hospital

Name:

Home phone number:

Office phone number:

Surviving a heart attack

Phone 999 immediately if you think you are having a heart attack or if you suspect someone else is having a heart attack. This means that you or they will get potentially life-saving treatment as soon as possible. Do not phone your GP if you think you or someone else is having a heart attack, you must phone 999 for an ambulance.

The sooner you get emergency treatment, the greater your chances of survival and the more of your heart muscle can be saved.

Some people delay phoning 999. They may ignore or be uncertain of the symptoms, not think that a heart attack can happen to them, or not want to make a fuss.

The first thing to do if you think you're having a heart attack is to phone 999 immediately for an ambulance.

You should then sit and rest while you wait for the ambulance to arrive.

If you are not allergic to aspirin and have some next to you, or if there is someone with you who can fetch them for you, chew an aspirin. However, if they are not nearby, the person with you should not go looking for aspirin, they should stay with you.

Do not get up and look for an aspirin. This may put unnecessary strain on your heart.

'Phone 999 immediately if you think you are having a heart attack or if you suspect someone else is having a heart attack.'

How is a heart attack diagnosed?

The ambulance staff will:

* Do an ECG.

* Give aspirin if not given already.

* Assess your symptoms and medical history.

* Give pain relief if needed and oxygen if your oxygen level is too low.

* Examine you and monitor your heart rate and blood pressure.

How is a heart attack treated?

Treatment of heart attacks includes:

- Medications and/or surgery to restore blood supply to your heart.

- Medications to decrease the need for oxygen by the heart's muscle.

- Medications to prevent abnormal heart rhythms.

The primary goal of treatment is to quickly restore blood flow and decrease damage to your heart muscle, a process called reperfusion. Delaying reperfusion may reduce the ability of your heart to pump blood in the future. In the future, if your heart is unable to pump sufficient blood you may develop heart failure, have a decreased ability to exercise and abnormal heart rhythms.

What to expect during recovery from a heart attack

If you have had a heart attack you will be monitored in the hospital. Arrhythmias, shortness of breath due to heart failure or recurrent chest pain are reasons for further therapy such as additional medications, coronary angioplasty or bypass surgery.

You will gradually increase your level of activity under observation. Before resuming full activity or work, several weeks may be needed for the heart muscle to heal.

- After a small heart attack (little damage to heart muscle), you may resume normal activities after two weeks. These activities include returning to work as well as normal sexual activity.

- After a moderate heart attack (moderate damage to heart muscle) you may gradually increase activity for up to four weeks.

- After a large heart attack (much damage to heart muscle) you may need a recovery period of six weeks or longer.

Cardiac rehabilitation (rehab) may begin during hospitalisation and continues after discharge. Cardiac rehab provides a long-term lifestyle programme tailored specifically for you and will help you and your family adjust to life following a heart attack.

How can a second heart attack be prevented?

- Take all prescribed medications and undergo recommended further testing.

- Stop smoking.

- Reduce excess weight, and exercise regularly.

- Control blood pressure and diabetes.

- Eat a healthy balanced diet.

Summing Up

A heart attack is a serious medical emergency. If you are at risk for a heart attack:

- Learn the heart attack warning signs.

- Have a heart attack survival plan.

- Phone 999 immediately if you think you are having a heart attack, or if you think someone else is.

- Carefully follow all your doctor's recommendations during recovery from a heart attack.

Chapter Eight

Eating For Your Heart

You can avoid heart problems in the future and prevent an existing heart condition from getting worse by adopting a heart-healthy lifestyle. A heart-healthy lifestyle involves maintaining a healthy diet. To establish your heart-healthy diet, make short-term and long-term goals to help you change your habits for good.

Eat well

What you eat can have a big impact on the health of your heart. A heart-healthy diet consists of protein (lean meat, fish, dairy products, vegetarian alternatives), unsaturated fat, carbohydrates (starchy foods such as bread and pasta), fruit and vegetables. It is low in saturated fat, salt and sugar. A healthy diet will help your heart by:

- Lowering your blood pressure.

- Increasing your good HDL cholesterol and decreasing your bad LDL cholesterol. Eating a heart-healthy diet can help to lower your cholesterol levels by 5-10% (British Heart Foundation: www.bhf.org.uk).

- Preventing blood clots that can lead to a heart attack.

- Keeping your body weight in a healthy range.

Fats

In particular, when establishing your heart-healthy diet, you should cut down on the total amount of fat you eat. For a heart-healthy diet, no more than 30% of your daily calories should come from fat.

You can calculate your fat intake by:

- Looking at the nutritional information for every item in your meals.

- Adding the fat grams from all your meals.

- Multiplying the number of fat grams by 9 (the number of calories in one gram of fat).

- Adding up all your meals' calories consumed for the day.

- Dividing your total number of fat calories by your total daily calories to determine your daily % of calories acquired from fat.

- For example: If you have eaten 45 grams of fat; that is 45 x 9 = 405 calories from fat. If your total calories for the day are 1,700; that is 405 divided by 1,700 = 24% of your calories are from fat.

Types of fat

For your heart-healthy diet, it is essential to eat fewer fats, but it is also important to eat the right types of fat. There are three main types of fat in foods including:

- Saturated fats contained in fatty meats, full-fat dairy products, butter, lard, cream, cheese and many processed and takeaway foods. It is important to avoid or eat less of these foods as saturated fats increase LDL cholesterol.

- Polyunsaturated fats contained in pure vegetable oils and spreads such as sunflower, corn and soya oils, margarines and some vegetables. These types of fat help to lower LDL, but they also lower HDL cholesterol.

- Monounsaturated fats contained in olive oil, rapeseed oil, avocados, nuts and seeds. These types of fats lower LDL and help to maintain levels of HDL cholesterol.

Trans fats

Another group of fats are trans fats. Trans fats are found in foods that contain hydrogenated fats or hydrogenated vegetable oils and may be as harmful to your heart as saturated fats. Hydrogenated fats and oils are usually found in processed foods as they improve the texture, flavour and shelf life of these products. Food manufacturers are not legally obliged to label their products as containing trans fats, but any product that contains hydrogenated fat or hydrogenated oil as an ingredient contains trans fats and should be avoided.

Omega-3 fats

Omega-3 fats are a particular type of polyunsaturated fat. Researchers believe omega-3 fats are important for a heart-healthy diet as they:

▨ Regulate blood clotting.

▨ Keep your heart beating regularly and protect the arteries which carry blood to your heart.

▨ Lower levels of triglycerides.

Omega-3 fats are found in oily fish such as salmon, sardines, mackerel, trout, fresh tuna, pilchards, kippers and herring. The Food Standards Agency (www. food.gov.uk) recommends we should eat at least one serving of oily fish each week. In addition, your body can make omega-3 fats from foods like rapeseed oil, walnut oil and soya.

Cholesterol

Foods such as liver, kidney, prawns and eggs contain more dietary cholesterol than many other foods. However, the cholesterol in food has little effect on our blood cholesterol levels. Consequently, there is no need to limit the amount of these foods you eat, unless your doctor or a dietitian has specifically advised you to do this.

Fibre

A heart-healthy diet should be rich in fibre. A high fibre diet contains wholegrain foods such as wholemeal bread, brown rice and wholegrain breakfast cereals. Fibre-rich foods are:

▨ Low in fat.

▨ Packed with vitamins and minerals.

In addition, soluble fibre, as found in some fruits, vegetables, oats, barley and pulses such as beans, lentils and peas is particularly good for your heart. Soluble fibre:

- May help to lower blood cholesterol levels. Soluble fibre binds cholesterol and prevents it from being reabsorbed into the bloodstream. This lowers the amount of cholesterol in the blood, therefore reducing the risk of heart disease.

- Forms a gel in the intestine which slows down the digestion and absorption of carbohydrates and keeps blood sugar levels steady. This prevents you from craving carbohydrates and eating high sugar, high fat foods such as biscuits, chocolate and cake.

Studies show that a high fibre diet can protect you from heart disease. For example, women who ate three servings of wholegrain foods a day were 30% less likely to suffer from heart disease.

'Women who ate three servings of wholegrain foods a day were 30% less likely to suffer from heart disease.'

Fruits and vegetables

Eating a diet packed with fruits and vegetables can also protect your heart. Health experts recommend eating 5 to 10 servings of different fruits and vegetables every day and as many different colours as possible. Eating different coloured fruits and vegetables provide you with a greater variety of nutrients.

Fruits and vegetables are:

- Low in fat.

- High in fibre.

- Packed with antioxidants.

Antioxidants protect against heart disease. Antioxidants include vitamins such as beta-carotene and vitamins C and E and naturally occurring plant chemicals called flavonoids. Antioxidants clean up chemicals called free radicals. Free radicals are harmful as they can change LDL cholesterol, which is already harmful, and actually speed up narrowing of arteries.

Soya

A diet that includes soya may help to protect you against heart disease. Soya provides both soluble fibre and isoflavones (from the flavonoid family). Including 25g of soya protein in a diet low in saturated fats can help lower total and LDL cholesterol. You can get this amount of soya protein by drinking around three glasses of soya milk a day or eating soya desserts, yogurt alternatives and creams. However, make sure you choose unsweetened varieties and check the nutrition information as these products may be high in calories.

Salt

To establish a heart-healthy diet you should try to reduce the amount of salt (sodium) you eat. Salt makes your body hold on to water, and the extra water stored in your body raises your blood pressure and puts strain on your heart. High sources of salt are found in many types of convenience and snack foods. Try to limit your use of salt in cooking and on your food. Use the table below (NHS choices – Your health, your choices www.nhs.uk) to make sure you are not eating too much salt.

Recommended Daily Salt Intake		Salt (1 level tsp = 6g)	Sodium (1 level tsp = 2g)
Healthy adult	Older than 18 years	2.3g	0.9g
Diagnosed with high blood pressure	18-50 yrs	1.5g	0.6g
	51-70 years	1.3g	0.5g
	Older than 70	1.2g	0.5g

Eating plans

There are several eating plans that are designed to help you establish a heart-healthy diet. For example:

- The Dietary Approaches to Stop Hypertension (high blood pressure) eating plan focuses on foods that are high in calcium, potassium and magnesium as these nutrients can lower blood pressure. The foods that are highest in these nutrients are fruits, vegetables, low-fat dairy products, nuts, seeds and beans. For more information see www.bloodpressure.org.uk/foods-dash.php.

- The Therapeutic Lifestyle Changes (TLC) diet is a cholesterol-lowering diet that lowers your LDL level and raises your HDL level enough to reduce your risk of heart disease. The TLC diet follows these dietary guidelines:

- Less than 7% of the day's total calories from saturated fat.

- 25-35% of the day's total calories from fat.

- Less than 200 milligrams of dietary cholesterol a day.

For more information see Your Guide to Lowering Your Cholesterol with TLC: Therapeutic Lifestyle Changes www.nhlbi.nih.gov/health/public/heart/chol/chol_tlc.pdf.

Before starting one of these eating plans always consult your doctor. In addition, a registered dietitian can help you change your eating habits and plan your menus.

Ideas for healthy eating

The following tables contain some ideas to help you establish a heart-healthy diet.

Meat, poultry, fish, dry beans, eggs and nuts	Limit the total amount of meat to 5 ounces or less per day.
	Choose chicken and turkey without skin or remove skin before eating.
	Eat fish, like cod, that has less saturated fat than either chicken or meat.
	Dry peas and beans and tofu are great meat substitutes.
	Add beans to a salad or make split pea or black bean soup.
	Limit egg yolks to no more than 2 yolks per week, including egg yolks in baked goods.
	Substitute egg whites for whole eggs.

Milk, yogurt, and cheese	Eat 2 to 3 servings per day of low fat or non-fat dairy products.
	Choose varieties that have 3 grams of fat or less per ounce, including low fat (1%) or non-fat cottage cheese.
	Buy frozen desserts that are lower in saturated fat, like low-fat frozen yogurt and sorbet.
	Try low-fat or non-fat sour cream or cream cheese blends.
	Make a dip for fruit from low-fat or non-fat vanilla yogurt and cinnamon.

Fats and oils	Replace saturated fats with unsaturated fat and limit the total amount of fats or oils.
	Use liquid vegetable oils that are high in unsaturated fats (canola, corn, olive, peanut, safflower, sesame, soybean, sunflower oils).
	Use margarine made with unsaturated liquid vegetable oils as the first ingredient.
	Limit butter and solid shortenings.
	Buy light or non-fat mayonnaise and salad dressing.

Fruits and vegetables	Eat at least 3 to 5 servings of fruits and vegetables each day.
	Buy fruits and vegetables to eat as snacks, desserts, salads, side dishes and main dishes.
	Add a variety of vegetables to meat stews or casseroles or make a vegetarian main dish.
	Make a stir-fry with lots of different vegetables.
	Make a baked potato. Serve baked potatoes with vegetables, such as broccoli, and toppings, such as low-fat cheese, chilli and refried beans. If you use toppings from a jar, be sure to choose low-sodium/salt varieties. It is better to make the toppings yourself from fresh ingredients. This can help increase your servings of vegetables.
	Combine a ready-made pizza crust with low fat mozzarella cheese and lots of vegetable toppings such as tomatoes, courgettes, spinach, carrots, cauliflower and onions.
	Snack on raw vegetables (carrots, broccoli, cauliflower, lettuce) and fruit.
	Season salads with herbs, spices, lemon juice, vinegar, fat-free or low-fat mayonnaise or salad dressing.
	Buy a vegetarian cookbook, and try some different recipes.

Breads, cereals, rice, pasta, and other grains	Eat 6 to 11 servings of foods from this group each day.
	Choose wholegrain breads, rolls and cereals.
	Buy dry cereals, most are low in fat, and limit high fat granola, muesli, and oat bran types made with coconut or coconut oil and nuts.
	Buy pasta and rice to use as entrees but eliminate the high fat sauces (butter, cheese, cream).
	Limit sweet baked goods that are made with lots of saturated fat.

Sweets and snacks	Choose sweets and snacks only every now and then.
	Buy snack foods low in fat.
	Some sweets and snacks may be low in fat, but most are not low in calories.
	To reduce sodium intake, look for low sodium or unsalted varieties.

Write down everything you eat every day. That way you can see how much of each food group you've eaten and where you need to add or cut back.

Summing Up

Your goal is to make changes to your diet that will benefit your heart health. These five steps can help:

■ Assess yourself and create your overall heart-healthy eating plan. What are your risk factors? Which changes would lower these risk factors?

■ Pick one area to start with. Write down one goal, including what you want to accomplish and the steps it takes to get you there. Try to come up with a timetable for making the changes.

■ Line up your resources and supporters. Doctors and dieticians can help with making changes to your diet.

■ Start with a few small healthy changes and make them part of your routine Perhaps you want to add more fruit and vegetables to your diet. You could start with adding an extra portion to one meal a day. Increase these changes every week.

■ Reward yourself and keep at it. Rewards can help you stay motivated and keep you moving onto the next change.

Chapter Nine

Lifestyle Changes
For Your Heart

Your lifestyle is your best defense against heart disease. Your lifestyle is something you can take responsibility for. With a few simple changes, including taking regular exercise, reducing your alcohol intake, stopping smoking and managing your stress, you can help your heart stay healthy.

Move well

Exercise can help prevent heart disease in most people, and just 30 minutes of moderate-intensity exercise, such as walking, most days of the week can improve your blood pressure and cholesterol levels, help you maintain a healthy weight and so substantially reduce your risk of heart disease. Inactive people have almost double the risk of dying from heart disease compared with people who are active.

NHS Choices (www.nhs.uk/Livewell/fitness/Pages/whybeactive.aspx) suggests adults should do at least 150 minutes (2 hours and 30 minutes) of moderate-intensity aerobic activity each week. Aerobic exercise is exercise that increases your need for oxygen and strengthens your heart and lungs. During aerobic exercise, your muscles demand more oxygen-rich blood and give off more carbon dioxide and other waste products. Therefore, your heart has to beat faster to keep up. When you follow an aerobic exercise plan, your heart grows stronger so it can meet your muscles' demands.

Moderate-intensity aerobic activity means you're working hard enough to raise your heart rate and break a sweat. If you are working at a moderate intensity you should still be able to talk but not sing the words to a song.

'Just 30 minutes of moderate-intensity exercise can substantially reduce your risk of heart disease.'

Examples of aerobic activities include:

Moderate Activity	Vigorous Activity
Bicycling (less than 10mph)	Aerobic dancing
Dancing	Basketball
Golf (on foot)	Bicycling (more than 10mph)
Hiking (flat ground)	Hiking (uphill)
Horseriding	Jogging/running fast (at least 5mph)
Roller skating	Jumping rope
Swimming	Stair climbing
Tennis (doubles)	Tennis (singles)
Walking moderately (3.5mph)	Walking briskly (4.5mph)
Weightlifting (moderate effort)	Weightlifting (vigorous effort)
Gardening (light)	Gardening (heavy)
	Football

You should also include strength training for in your healthy heart exercise programme. Strength training is the process of exercising with progressively heavier resistance. It is also known as weightlifting, weight training or body building. Strength training increases the size and strength of your muscles. Your muscles use calories even at rest, so the more muscle you have the more calories you use. So, building muscle can help you with weight loss and weight maintenance.

As you become more physically active you can track the beneficial effects of exercise on your heart by tracking your heart rate during activity. The activity level most beneficial for your heart is your 'target heart rate zone' which uses 50-75% of your maximum heart rate. During the first few months of your exercise programme, aim to reach 50% of your maximum heart rate. As you become fitter, slowly build up to 75%. To find your target heart rate zone find the age closest to you on the table below. For example, if you are 45, your target heart rate zone is 90-135 beats per minute.

Age	Target Heart Rate Zone (beats per minute): 50-75%	Maximum Heart Rate (beats per minute): 100%
20	100-150	200
25	98-146	195
30	95-142	190
35	93-138	185
40	90-135	180
45	88-131	175
50	85-127	170
55	83-123	165
60	80-120	160
65	78-116	155
70	75-113	150

To find out whether you are within your target heart rate zone, take your pulse immediately after finishing your activity by placing the tips of your fingers on the inside of your wrist just below the base of your thumb; count your pulse for 10 seconds and multiply by six. If your pulse falls within your target zone your activity is benefitting your heart. If you are outside your target zone, move faster (if lower) or slower (if higher) next time you exercise.

Some people should take medical advice before starting or increasing physical activity. Check with your doctor if you are:

- Starting an exercise plan and have been inactive for a long period of time.
- Over 50 years old and not used to moderate activity.
- Have a heart condition, have had chest pain within the last month or have had a heart attack.
- Have a parent or sibling who developed heart disease.
- Tend to lose your balance or become dizzy.

- Feel breathless after mild exertion.
- Are on any type of medication.

A heart-healthy exercise plan

Before you start exercising, always make sure you have:

- The right shoes.
- The correct clothing.
- Wear appropriate protective gear such as helmets, reflective clothing if exercising in the evening and sunscreen and a hat if exercising outside.

Here is a simple sample workout plan. As you become fitter gradually increase the time spent on each activity.

Day	Activity
Monday	30-45 mins: brisk walking
Tuesday	20-45 mins: strength training
Wednesday	30-45 mins: brisk walking or biking
Thursday	30-45 mins: brisk walking or biking
Friday	20-45 mins: strength training
Saturday	30-60 mins: swimming, playing tennis or golf (without a cart)
Sunday	Rest day

Stop exercising immediately and consult your doctor if you:

- Have pain or pressure in the left or middle part of your chest, or in the left side of your neck, left shoulder or left arm.
- Feel dizzy or sick.
- Break out in a cold sweat.
- Have muscle cramps.
- Feel sharp pain in your joints, feet, ankles or bones.
- Notice that your heart starts racing or beating irregularly.

Other heart-healthy lifestyle changes

Alcohol

Drinking alcohol can increase your risk for heart disease if you have high blood pressure, diabetes, obesity or high triglycerides. Drinking alcohol can worsen your condition if you have heart failure, cardiomyopathy, arrhythmia or are taking medications.

If you drink alcohol, limit yourself to one or two standard drinks a day, to a weekly maximum of nine for women and 14 for men. For more information see www.patient.co.uk/health/Recommended-Safe-Limits-of-Alcohol.

One drink equals:

- 341 mL/12 oz (1 bottle) of regular strength beer (5% alcohol).

- 142 mL/5 oz wine (12% alcohol).

- 43 mL/1 1/2 oz spirits (40% alcohol).

To moderate your alcohol intake:

- Talk to your doctor about the risks of drinking alcohol.

- If you don't drink, don't start.

- If you do drink, wait at least one hour between drinks, and alternate alcoholic drinks with water or juice.

- Avoid drinking excessively or getting drunk.

- Seek help from a support group such as Drinkline (www.drinking.nhs.uk).

Smoking

Smoking is a risk factor for heart disease, as it is a major cause of atherosclerosis and heart attack. In fact, if you smoke, your risk of heart attack greatly increases with the number of cigarettes you smoke, and you continue to increase your risk of heart attack the longer you smoke. If you smoke a pack of cigarettes a day you have more than twice the risk of a heart attack than non-smokers.

There is no safe amount of smoking. If you smoke you should do all you can to become smoke-free. Once you become smoke-free you will immediately reduce your risk of heart disease. The sooner you become smoke-free, the sooner your body can start to recover, and it doesn't take long to see the effects:

- Within 48 hours, your chances of having a heart attack start to go down and your sense of smell and taste begin to improve.

- Within 1 year, your risk of suffering a smoking-related heart attack is cut in half.

- Within 15 years, your risk of heart attack is the same as someone who never smoked at all.

Being smoke-free can be difficult. Start by identifying your smoking triggers, and then break the connection between smoking and your routines. Make your home and car smoke-free zones and set a date to stop smoking. Many people find support groups and hotlines helpful when stopping smoking (e.g., NHS SmokeFree www.smokefree.nhs.uk). Knowing that someone out there understands and shares your struggle can help you stay committed to being smoke free.

See *Stop Smoking - The Essential Guide* (Need2Know) for help and advice on becoming smoke-free.

'The sooner you become smoke-free, the sooner your body can start to recover, and it doesn't take long to see the effects.'

Stress

Stress can increase your risk of heart disease. If you have high levels of stress or prolonged stress you may have higher blood cholesterol, increased blood pressure or be more prone to developing atherosclerosis. If your life is stressful, it can be difficult to lead a healthy lifestyle. Instead of being physically active to relieve stress, you may overeat, eat unhealthy foods, and consume too much alcohol, or smoke.

Responding to stress with anger can also be harmful, since it increases your heart rate and blood pressure levels, which can increase your chance of having a heart attack. People who are prone to anger are also more likely to turn to unhealthy behaviours such as smoking, excessive alcohol consumption and overeating.

Stress can be caused by a physical or emotional change, or a change in your environment that requires you to adjust or respond. Things that make you feel stressed are called 'stressors'.

Stressors can be minor hassles, major lifestyle changes, or a combination of both and include illness, death of loved one, problems in personal relationships or at work, pregnancy, moving house and financial problems. Being able to identify stressors in your life and releasing the tension they cause are the keys to managing stress.

The first step towards reducing the stress in your life is to identify your stressors; the next step is to learn techniques that can help you cope with stress. There are many techniques you can use to manage stress. Some of these you can learn yourself, while other techniques may require the guidance of a trained therapist.

Some common techniques for coping with stress include:

- Eat and drink sensibly. Avoid alcohol which can add to your stress.

- Assert yourself. Being assertive allows you to stand up for your rights and beliefs while respecting those of others.

- Stop smoking. Smoking can actually bring on more stress symptoms.

- Exercise regularly. Exercise has been shown to release natural substances called endorphins that help you feel better and maintain a positive attitude.

- Relax every day. Try deep breathing, yoga, relax to music or learn stress-reduction techniques from a therapist.

- Manage your time. Your life may be filled with too many demands and too little time. Effective time-management skills involve asking for help when appropriate, setting priorities, pacing yourself and taking time out for yourself.

- Examine your values and live by them. The more your actions reflect your beliefs, the better you will feel, no matter how busy your life is.

- Set realistic goals and expectations.

- Self-esteem. When you are feeling overwhelmed, remind yourself of what you do well. Have a healthy sense of self-esteem.

- Get enough rest. Even with proper diet and exercise, you can't fight stress effectively without rest. You need time to recover from exercise and stressful events. The time you spend resting should be long enough to relax your mind as well as your body. Taking a nap in the middle of the day may help you reduce stress.

- Seek help from a counsellor from organisations such as the British Association for Counselling and Psychotherapy www.bacp.co.uk.

For more information on handling stress, take a look at *Stress – The Essential Guide* by Frances Ive, Need2Know.

Summing Up

- Your lifestyle can make a huge difference to the health of your heart.

- An active lifestyle can significantly reduce your chance of developing heart disease.

- Enjoy alcohol in moderation.

- If you smoke, stopping smoking is the biggest step you can take to reduce your risk of heart disease.

- Take steps to manage your stress.

- Talk with your doctor and see if you can reduce your risk for heart disease or manage an existing condition by adopting a heart-healthy lifestyle.

Chapter Ten

Women and Heart Disease

How does heart disease affect women?

It is a myth that more men die of heart disease than women. In fact, 1 in 3 women die of heart disease. Heart disease is the most common cause of death for women in the UK and 3 times more women die from heart disease than breast cancer. According to the British Heart Foundation (www.bhf.org.uk), there are over 1 million women in the UK living with heart disease. However, as a woman, if you are aware of your risks and take steps to control your risks or an existing heart condition, you can successfully protect the health of your heart. For more information see Women's Health Concern (www.womens-health-concern.org)

Specific risk factors for heart disease in women

Women and men generally have the same risk factors for heart disease, but some risk factors, such as diabetes, stress and sleep apnoea may affect women differently than men, and some risk factors, including birth control pills and menopause, only affect women.

Diabetes and prediabetes

Diabetes is a disease in which the blood sugar level in your body is too high. Your blood sugar level is controlled by the hormone insulin which helps move sugar from your blood into your cells. Your cells use sugar to give you energy.

If you have diabetes, your body does not make enough insulin or does not use its insulin properly. Over time, high blood sugar levels can lead to plaque build-up in your arteries. Prediabetes is a condition in which your blood sugar level is higher than normal, but not as high as it is in diabetes. Prediabetes puts you at higher risk for both diabetes and heart disease.

Heart disease is an important cause of illness among women with diabetes; rates are 3-7 times higher among 45-64 year-old women with diabetes than among those without diabetes, and diabetes raises the risk of heart disease in women more than men. The reason for this difference between men and women is not fully understood, but diabetes may have a greater effect on risk factors for heart disease in women than in men.

Depression

Stress and depression may play a role in causing heart disease. Stress can cause your arteries to narrow, increase your blood pressure and your risk for having a heart attack. Stress can also cause you to overeat foods that are high in fat and sugar and to start smoking, all of which increase your risk for heart attack. If you are depressed, you are two or three times more likely to develop heart disease than people who are not. In addition, depression makes it difficult to maintain a healthy lifestyle and follow recommended treatment. Depression as a risk for heart disease is of particular concern in women, as depression is twice as common in women as in men, and mental stress and depression affect women's hearts more than men's.

Sleep apnoea

Sleep apnoea is a common disorder that causes you to pause your breathing for a few seconds to minutes or take shallow breaths while you sleep. These pauses or shallow breaths may often occur 5-30 times or more in one hour. You will start breathing again normally after the pause or shallow breaths, sometimes with a loud snort or choking sound. Major signs of sleep apnoea are snoring and daytime sleepiness.

When you stop breathing, there is a lack of oxygen which triggers your body's stress hormones. This causes blood pressure to rise and makes your blood more likely to clot. Untreated sleep apnoea can raise your risk for high blood pressure, diabetes and heart disease. Women are especially likely to develop sleep apnoea after the menopause.

Oral contraceptives

If you take the oral contraceptive pill, you may have a slightly increased risk for heart disease. This is because the oral contraceptive pill can increase your C-reactive protein (CRP) levels. Elevated CRP levels are associated with a condition called 'low grade inflammation' which can increase your risk for plaque build-up. Researchers have found a 20-30% increase in arterial plaque in two big arteries in the neck and leg for every 10 years a woman uses the oral contraceptive pill. This means your increased risk for heart disease remains with you even after you stop taking the pill. In addition, if you use the oral contraceptive pill, you are more likely to have high 'bad' (LDL) cholesterol relative to 'good' (HDL) cholesterol. However, if you use the oral contraceptive pill it is not necessary to worry. Just be sure to follow a heart-healthy lifestyle by eating a healthier diet, getting more exercise, not smoking and controlling cholesterol.

Menopause

Women who have reached the menopause have an increased risk of developing heart disease. It is not clear why this happens, but it may be related to a drop in the hormone estrogen which occurs in women at menopause. Hormone replacement therapy (HRT) was thought to reduce the risk of heart disease for menopausal women. However, recent studies have shown that HRT may increase the risk of heart disease for some women. Women should always talk to their health-care providers to decide if hormone therapy is right for them.

Heart attacks in women

Symptoms

In the past, research on heart attacks has mainly focused on men. However, recent studies show that the symptoms of heart attacks in women are different from those in men.

The signs of heart attacks in women often go unnoticed or are assumed to be due to other health problems or drug side effects. Women often believe the symptoms will go away on their own. This means that women sometimes do not get the health care they need to prevent complications or death from heart disease.

Women often report symptoms up to one month before a heart attack. Chest pain is the most common symptom in both sexes, but women may also experience these other symptoms:

- Unusual fatigue that gets worse with activity.
- Difficulty breathing.
- Heartburn that is unrelieved by antacids.
- Nausea and/or vomiting that is unrelieved by antacids.
- Anxiety.
- Tightening and pain in the chest that may extend into the neck, jaws and shoulders.
- General feeling of weakness.
- Paleness.
- Sweating.

Some women only have a few of these symptoms, while others may have all of them. Symptoms may come and go. If you have any of these symptoms and think you may be having a heart attack, you *must* call 999 or go to the nearest hospital.

Rehabilitation

If you have had a heart attack, or a treatment such as heart surgery or angioplasty, you will be offered a place on a cardiac rehabilitation (rehab) programme. Cardiac rehab has been found to reduce your risk of dying from heart disease and improve your long-term health. It helps you to recover and get back to your usual activities.

According to the British Heart Foundation (www.bhf.org.uk), women are less likely than men to attend cardiac rehab. Some women are embarrassed if there are fewer women than men in the group. Others may feel that they are too busy with family or other commitments. But cardiac rehab is very important for your recovery and the benefits and support you receive far outweigh any inconvenience or embarrassment you may feel.

You can find out about your nearest cardiac rehab programme by asking your GP or visiting www.cardiac-rehabilitation.net.

Pregnancy and heart disease

Women at risk for heart disease or with an existing heart condition require special care if they become pregnant.

Changes to the heart and blood vessels with pregnancy

During pregnancy, changes occur to your heart and blood vessels. These can add stress to your body and increase the workload of your heart. These changes are normal during pregnancy, as they ensure that your baby is getting enough oxygen and nutrients. However, if you are at risk of heart disease or have a heart condition, you may need to take special precautions before and during pregnancy, as your risk factors or condition may cause complications during pregnancy. In addition, some heart conditions may be identified during pregnancy.

You should be evaluated by a heart specialist before you start planning a pregnancy if you have:

- Hypertension (high blood pressure) or high cholesterol.

- Any type of heart disease.

- Ever had a heart attack.

- Poor heart function, for example as measured by the amount of blood pumped out of the left ventricle during each heartbeat (ejection fraction). A normal ejection fraction is 50-70%. If you have an ejection fraction of less than 40% you should consult a heart specialist.

Based on your risk factors or condition, your heart specialist will talk to you about the safety of pregnancy and discuss potential complications to you and your baby during pregnancy.

By preparing for pregnancy and following up regularly with your heart specialist during pregnancy, most women with a heart condition can safely become pregnant and have a healthy baby.

'By preparing for pregnancy and following up regularly with your heart specialist during pregnancy, most women with a heart condition can safely become pregnant and have a healthy baby.'

Pre-existing heart conditions and pregnancy

- Arrhythmias and pregnancy: Abnormal heartbeats (arrhythmias) during pregnancy are common. Arrhythmias may develop for the first time because of pregnancy or arrhythmias may be the result of a previously unknown heart condition. Most of the time, no treatment is required. If symptoms develop, your doctor may order tests to determine the cause of the arrhythmias.

- Valve disease and pregnancy: If you have valve disease you need to be evaluated by a heart specialist before planning a pregnancy. In some cases, surgery and medication to correct the valve may be recommended before pregnancy.

- Congenital heart conditions and pregnancy: If you have been diagnosed with a congenital heart defect, a heart specialist will evaluate your heart condition before you plan a pregnancy. In general, most women with a congenital heart defect, especially those who have had corrective surgery, can safely become pregnant.

Heart conditions that may develop during pregnancy

High blood pressure (hypertension)

About 6-8% of women develop high blood pressure or pregnancy-induced hypertension (PIH) during pregnancy. PIH is a complication characterised by high blood pressure, swelling due to fluid retention and protein in the urine.

PIH is related to pre-eclampsia. Pre-eclampsia is characterised by a rise in blood pressure and excess protein in the urine during the second half of pregnancy. These signs usually go away after delivery. However, pre-eclampsia:

- Increases your risk of developing high blood pressure later in life.

- Is linked to an increased lifetime risk of heart disease. If you had pre-eclampsia during pregnancy, you're twice as likely to develop heart disease as women who haven't had the condition. You're also more likely to develop heart disease earlier in life. The more severe your pre-eclampsia was, the greater your risk for heart disease.

- Pre-eclampsia is a heart disease risk factor that you can't control. However, if you've had the condition, you should take extra care to eat a healthier diet, get more exercise, stop smoking and control your cholesterol.

Heart murmur

Sometimes, a heart murmur may develop as a result of the increase in blood volume that occurs during pregnancy. In most cases, the murmur is harmless but it could mean there's a problem with a heart valve. Your doctor should evaluate your condition

Summing Up

- It is never too late to protect your heart. Look at some of the facts in the table below and decide to take action.

- You must protect your heart or prevent your heart disease from becoming worse.

- Why not visit your GP and get a health check or identify some risk factors you can improve and start working on them.

- If you suspect you have any symptoms of heart disease, deal with them quickly.

- If you suffer from heart disease, make the most of the benefits and support on offer so you can make the best recovery possible.

Women and heart disease: The facts

- There are more than 1 million women in the UK living with coronary heart disease.

- 40,000 women in the UK die from coronary heart disease each year.

- Nearly a million women in the UK suffer from angina.

- Nearly half a million women in the UK have had a heart attack.

- 430,000 women in the UK are living with heart failure.

- One in five women in the UK smoke, doubling their risk of having a heart attack.

- 30% of women in England and Scotland have high blood pressure.

- 60% of women in England and Scotland have cholesterol levels >5 mmol/l.

- More than 50% of women in the UK are overweight or obese.

- Less than 30% of women in England exercise enough to protect their heart.

- 30% of women in the UK drink more than the recommended amount of alcohol.

Source: Women and heart disease British Heart Foundation www.bhf.org.uk/women

Glossary

Angiotensin–converting enzyme
(ACE) inhibitors are a type of heart medication that cause your blood vessels to relax and widen (dilate).

Arrhythmias
Arrhythmias are heart palpitations (racing or slow heartbeats you are aware of) that may occur if you do not have heart disease but are at risk for heart disease or as a symptom of heart disease.

Atherectomy
An atherectomy is a surgical procedure used to help remove plaque from blood vessels other than coronary arteries.

Atherosclerosis
Atherosclerosis is a condition that occurs when plaque builds up in your arteries. Plaque is made up of fat, cholesterol, calcium, and other substances found in your blood.

Atresia
Heart valve disease when a heart valve lacks an opening for blood to pass through.

Atria
The left and right atria are the upper chambers of your heart.

Beta blockers
Beta-blockers are a type of heart medication that decrease the activity of your heart and cause your heart to beat with less force.

Body mass index
Body mass index (BMI) is a measure of body fat based on height and weight that applies to adult men and women.

Bradycardia
Bradycardia occurs when your heart beats too slowly and may be a symptom of heart disease.

Calcium channel blockers
Calcium channel blockers are a type of heart medication that relax blood vessels and increase the supply of blood and oxygen to your heart while decreasing its workload.

Cardiac arrest
A cardiac arrest happens when your heart stops pumping blood around your body.

Cardiac catheterisation
Cardiac catheterisation, also called coronary angiogram, is a test to find out if you have atherosclerosis.

Cardiac computed tomography
Cardiac computed tomography is a heart-imaging test used to visualise your heart and blood vessels with or without contrast dye.

Cardiac pacemaker
A cardiac pacemaker is an artificial pacemaker that takes over the role of your heart's natural pacemaker.

Cardiomyopathy
Cardiomyopathy is a disease that changes the structure of the muscle tissue in your heart, or makes it weaker, so it's less able to pump blood efficiently.

Carotid arteries
Carotid arteries are blood vessels in your neck that carry blood and oxygen to your brain.

Cholesterol
Cholesterol is a soft, waxy substance found among the fats in your bloodstream and in all your body's cells. It is important for the healthy functioning of your body.

Congenital heart disease
Congenital heart defects are problems with your heart's structure that are present at birth.

Coronary angioplasty
Coronary angioplasty is a type of heart surgery that improves flow of blood to your heart through coronary arteries that have become narrowed.

Coronary artery disease
Coronary artery disease (CAD) is the most common type of heart disease, and is the leading cause of heart attacks. When you have CAD, your coronary arteries become hard and narrow as plaque builds up inside them.

Coronary bypass surgery
Coronary bypass surgery can be used to treat heart disease when your coronary arteries are blocked.

Cyanosis
Cyanosis is the bluish discolouration of the skin and the membranes in your mouth and nose and may be a symptom of heart disease.

Diabetes
Diabetes is a problem associated with the way our bodies use digested food for energy. Diabetes develops when your body does not make enough insulin, or the cells in your muscles, liver and fat do not use insulin properly, or both. As a result, the amount of glucose in your blood increases while your cells are starved of energy.

Digitalis
Digitalis is a type of heart medication that can be helpful if you have heart failure or an irregular heartbeat.

Diuretics
Diuretics are a type of heart medication that get rid of unneeded water and salt which decreases blood volume and makes it easier for your heart to pump.

Dyspnea
Dyspnea is a term for shortness of breath.

Echocardiogram
An echocardiogram is a test that checks for how your heart is functioning and may determine the presence of many types of heart disease.

Electrocardiogram
An electrocardiogram (ECG) is a test that checks for problems with the electrical activity of your heart.

Endocarditis

Endocarditis is an infection of the inner lining of your heart chambers and valves. This lining is called the endocardium.

Heart attack

A heart attack is a serious medical emergency in which the supply of blood to your heart is suddenly blocked, usually by a blood clot.

Heart block

Heart block is when you have a very slow heartbeat resulting in an inadequate blood and oxygen supply reaching your brain.

Heart transplant

A heart transplant is surgery to remove your diseased heart and replace it with a healthy heart from a deceased donor.

Heart valve replacement

Heart valve replacement is a type of surgery that is performed to repair or replace a valve in your heart that is leaking or narrowed and not working properly.

Hypertension

High blood pressure.

Lipoproteins – High-density lipoproteins and low-density lipoprotein

Lipoproteins, low-density lipoprotein (LDL) and high-density lipoprotein (HDL), carry cholesterol through your blood. High levels of LDL increase your risk of heart disease and heart attack as they can increase the build-up of cholesterol in your artery walls causing atherosclerosis. HDL reduces the risk of heart disease as it carries cholesterol away.

Magnetic resonance imaging

Magnetic resonance imaging (MRI) uses large magnets and radio frequency waves to produce pictures of the inside of your body.

Modifiable risk factors

Modifiable risk factors are unhealthy lifestyle choices that can be improved upon.

Nitrates

Nitrates are a type of heart medication that can improve the blood flow to your heart and can relieve and prevent angina pain.

Non-modifiable risk factors

Non-modifiable risk factors are risk factors that cannot be changed, such as age, gender, race/ethnicity and family history.

Nuclear scan

A nuclear heart scan is a test that checks for coronary heart disease, damage to your heart, and how well your heart is functioning.

Oedema

Oedema is swelling or puffiness of your ankles, legs, eyes, chest or belly, and may be a symptom of heart disease.

Palpitations

Palpitations are heartbeats you are aware of.

Pre-eclampsia

Pre-eclampsia is a condition in pregnancy related to pregnancy-induced hypertension. Pre-eclampsia is characterised by a rise in blood pressure and excess protein in the urine during the second half of pregnancy.

Pregnancy-induced hypertension

Pregnancy-induced hypertension is a complication of pregnancy characterised by high blood pressure, swelling due to fluid retention and protein in the urine.

Prolapse

Prolapse is when the flaps of the valve flop or bulge back into an upper heart chamber during a heartbeat. This leads to regurgitation, or backflow, as blood leaks back into the chambers rather than flowing forward through your heart or into an artery.

Pulmonary oedema or pulmonary congestion

Pulmonary oedema or pulmonary congestion is a condition characterised by fluid leaking from your bloodstream into your lungs.

Reperfusion

Reperfusion is a treatment that restores blood flow and decreases damage to your heart muscle.

Sinoatrial node

The sinoatrial node (SAN) is your heart's natural pacemaker that causes your heart to pump.

Stenosis

Heart valve disease when the flaps of a heart valve thicken, stiffen or fuse together.

Stress test

A stress test is a test that checks how your heart performs while your heart is stressed such as during exercise or due to the drug dobutamine.

Tachycardia

Tachycardia occurs when your heart beats too quickly and may be a symptom of heart disease.

Target heart rate zone

The activity level most beneficial for your heart is your 'target heart rate zone' which uses 50-75% of your maximum heart rate.

Triglyceride

Triglycerides are a common type of fat in the body.

Vasovagal syncope

Vasovagal syncope is a common cause of dizziness and lightheadedness.

Ventricles

The left and right ventricles are the lower chambers of your heart.

Help List

Act in Time to Heart Attack Signs

www.nhlbi.nih.gov/actintime

A website full of useful information designed as part of a campaign to increase awareness of the need to act fast when someone may be having a heart attack.

BBC Health

www.bbc.co.uk/health/

BBC Health is an informative website full of news, advice and links to give you information about the causes, symptoms and treatments of hundreds of health conditions.

Blood Pressure Association

FREEPOST LON 17815, 60 Cranmer Terrace, London SW17 0QS
Tel: 02087724994
www.bpassoc.org.uk

The Blood Pressure Association (BPA) is the UK charity dedicated to lowering the nation's blood pressure to prevent disability and death from stroke and heart disease. The vision of the BPA is that everyone will know their blood pressure numbers, in the same way that they know their height or weight, and take steps to keep them healthy both now and in the future. Sir David Attenborough is patron of the Blood Pressure Association and the chairman is Graham MacGregor, Professor of Cardiovascular Medicine, a leading expert in high blood pressure.

Bloodpressure (.org.uk)

www.bloodpressure.org.uk

A useful website with articles and books giving information about blood pressure and how to maintain yours for a healthy heart.

BootsWebMD

www.webmd.boots.com

BootsWebMD is a website that provides health information for the general public on the Internet. BootsWebMD provides credible information and in-depth reference material about health subjects that matter. BootsWebMD is a source of original and timely health information and features material from providers like the British Medical Journal and NHS Choices.

British Association for Counselling and Psychotherapy

01455 883300

www.bacp.co.uk

This organisation can help you to find a suitable counsellor in your area

British Heart Foundation

www.bhf.org.uk

The British Heart Foundation provides information and support for people with heart conditions and those who wish to look after their heart health. BHF has a Heart Helpline that can answer your questions on everything heart-related, and a Heart Matters service that offers free support and information for people looking to improve their heart health.

Diabetes UK

0845 120 2960

www.diabetes.org.uk

Diabetes UK is the largest organisation in the UK working for people with diabetes, funding research, campaigning and helping people live with the condition. Diabetes UK provides a comprehensive website with lots if information.

Drinkline

0800 917 8282

www.patient.co.uk

Drinkline provides confidential information, advice and support about drinking and drinking problems.

Food Standards Agency

www.food.gov.uk

The Food Standards Agency is responsible for food safety and food hygiene across the UK. The Food Standards Agency website contains all the latest Food Standards Agency news, food alerts, consultations, science, research and regulatory information.

NHS Blood and Transplant

www.nhsbt.nhs.uk/index.asp

NHS Blood and Transplant (NHSBT) manages the national voluntary donation system for blood, tissues, organs and stem cells turning these precious donations into products that can be used safely to the benefit of the patient. HSBT supplies around 2 million units of blood a year to hospitals in England and north Wales, and last year received 3,500 organ and 4,000 tissue donations and banked 2,200 cord blood units from across the UK.

NHS Choices

www.nhs.uk

NHS Choices is the UK's biggest health website. It provides a comprehensive health information service that puts you in control of your health care. The website helps you make choices about your health, from decisions about your lifestyle, such as smoking, drinking and exercise, to finding and using NHS services in England. NHS Choices includes around 20,000 regularly updated articles. There are also hundreds of thousands of entries in more than 50 directories that you can use to find and choose health services in England.

NHS SmokeFree

0800 022 4 332
www.smokefree.nhs.uk

This organisation will help you find your local NHS stop smoking service.

Patient.co.uk

www.patient.co.uk

Patient.co.uk is one of the most trusted medical resources in the UK, supplying evidence based information on a wide range of medical and health topics to patients and health professionals.

Women's Health Concern

01628 478 473
www.womens-health-concern.org
Women's Health Concern (WHC) provides an independent service to advise, reassure and educate women about their health concerns, to enable them to work in partnership with their own medical practitioners and health advisers. WHC offers unbiased information by telephone, email, in print, online and through conferences, seminars and symposia.

Need - 2 - Know

Available Titles Include ...

Allergies A Parent's Guide
ISBN 978-1-86144-064-8 £8.99

Autism A Parent's Guide
ISBN 978-1-86144-069-3 £8.99

Blood Pressure The Essential Guide
ISBN 978-1-86144-067-9 £8.99

Dyslexia and Other Learning Difficulties
A Parent's Guide ISBN 978-1-86144-042-6 £8.99

Bullying A Parent's Guide
ISBN 978-1-86144-044-0 £8.99

Epilepsy The Essential Guide
ISBN 978-1-86144-063-1 £8.99

Your First Pregnancy The Essential Guide
ISBN 978-1-86144-066-2 £8.99

Gap Years The Essential Guide
ISBN 978-1-86144-079-2 £8.99

Secondary School A Parent's Guide
ISBN 978-1-86144-093-8 £9.99

Primary School A Parent's Guide
ISBN 978-1-86144-088-4 £9.99

Applying to University The Essential Guide
ISBN 978-1-86144-052-5 £8.99

ADHD The Essential Guide
ISBN 978-1-86144-060-0 £8.99

Student Cookbook – Healthy Eating The Essential Guide
ISBN 978-1-86144-069-3 £8.99

Multiple Sclerosis The Essential Guide
ISBN 978-1-86144-086-0 £8.99

Coeliac Disease The Essential Guide
ISBN 978-1-86144-087-7 £9.99

Special Educational Needs A Parent's Guide
ISBN 978-1-86144-116-4 £9.99

The Pill An Essential Guide
ISBN 978-1-86144-058-7 £8.99

University A Survival Guide
ISBN 978-1-86144-072-3 £8.99

View the full range at **www.need2knowbooks.co.uk**.
To order our titles call **01733 898103**, email **sales@n2kbooks.com** or visit the website. Selected ebooks available online.

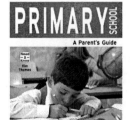
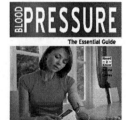
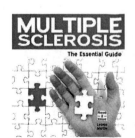

Need - 2 - Know, Remus House, Coltsfoot Drive, Peterborough, PE2 9BF

HEART DISEASE

The Essential Guide

Dr Jane Mijovic-Kondejewski

Heart Disease – The Essential Guide is also available in accessible formats for people with any degree of visual impairment. The large print edition and eBook (with accessibility features enabled) are available from Need2Know. Please let us know if there are any special features you require and we will do our best to accommodate your needs.

First published in Great Britain in 2012 by
Need2Know
Remus House
Coltsfoot Drive
Peterborough
PE2 9BF
Telephone 01733 898103
Fax 01733 313524
www.need2knowbooks.co.uk